The Gift of the
INDIGO

A Journey With Child Protective Services

LAURA DESISTO

Excerpts by Hali Sarah Parsons

© Laura Desisto 2017

Print ISBN: 978-1-54391-587-7

eBook ISBN: 978-1-54391-588-4

To Z, M and P with only the deepest love a mother can impart

FOREWORD

I felt urged by my angels to write a book. The thought had come to me several times in different ways. I know it's important to follow your inner guidance, so I finally gave in and decided to try.

The next morning when I got into my car to go to work, the word "Indigo" came into my head. Starre, my third and the most challenging child, had spoken to me of this word before. We Chambers' girls have been true believers in the presence of angels here on earth. Through our developing thought processes and discovering of metaphysics or so-called "new age" readings, we had discovered a wonderful earth angel named Doreen Virtue. When Starre had gone to Los Angeles to attend college, she actually met Doreen at a workshop and was able to speak with her briefly. Doreen had told Starre that she was an indigo. It made sense to me to use this in the title of the book. Sure enough confirmation came to me instantly by way of the first song that played when I turned on the radio. It was called "Closer to Fine" sung by the *Indigo Girls*! I started to get excited.

This is a true story written from a mom's (that's me) point of view. The names have been changed to protect the innocent. I am fond of soliciting a slight balance of clairsentience[1] to provoke raw emotions of the heart in my writings, so readers are able to remember who they are and whence they came from. Sometimes when thoroughly grounded and open to the universal energy, I'm able to perceive what I conclude to be a person's energy, which I label their "essence."

The way I see it, Starre, my youngest cherub has returned to the earth just to resolve a past life karma and accept a very challenging life of heartbreak and letting go. She writes, "Some things are permanent; some choices we make are preconceived for us to live out our purpose. The characteristics we agree to will not allow us to make certain choices at will. Thus, we create experiments that will bring force therein." Her responsibility to work through these challenges and life lessons are to be an important part of her growth on a spiritual level. It has become my opinion that one of her lessons may be learning to love herself unconditionally and hopefully to employ that self-love in making responsible life choices. This is an existence she and her loved ones chose while in the spiritual realm and before rebirth, as we are all eternal souls. All of us who know Starre have acknowledged and accepted our roles in being a part of her life while simultaneously working through our own lessons. This is divine planning.

Starre came as a surprise; she was "unplanned." Her dad and I never expected to be pregnant again. We had a boy and a girl already and were starting to drift apart somewhat. I really didn't know what was wrong with me as I remember it. I wasn't feeling very well and had decided to go to the doctors. A few days later I was contacted by phone and given the news—I was pregnant! Somewhat dumbstruck, I didn't tell her dad for a couple of months, like I said we were drifting apart after thirteen years of marriage. When I did tell him, I just blurted it out and ran out of the room. Doug,

---

[1] While there are five physical senses there are also four "clairs" or intuitive senses that we all have whether developed or not. Clairsentience is that of feeling energies or emotions. Clairaudience is that of hearing. Claircognizance is that of knowing from within, and clairvoyance is of seeing.

one of the thirteen siblings was elated with the news, completely the opposite of what I expected.

Starre Grace Chambers was born on April 24, 1990. We were thrilled with our new little bundle, our marriage was rekindled; she was our little angel. She brought so much bliss to everyone in our family. Her grandparents would come downstairs almost every night to cuddle her. Her older brother, Sam, and sister, Sunny, felt the same. They loved to help with her in any way. She was her dad's pride and joy; thus, her life began.

Starre was not like our first two children. She was tagged a spitfire by some as she always followed the beat of a different drum. Her carefree childhood days were alive with freedom and creativity. She loved to pose for pictures and she loved little bugs. I had gone back to work when she was ten months old because it was getting stagnant with her dad and myself both not working. Her dad—Doug—was tall and handsome. He was a hard worker and could do just about every type of construction job; but having been out of work, he stayed home with our little angel. Growing up with her dad's laid back parenting skills gave Starre the autonomy she needed to develop into the free spirit of who she was to become.

Her school years were marked with apprehension that her creativity was causing her to step out of the lines and this was not acceptable by most of the strict teachers at Cove Elementary. They wanted all their ducks in a row, and Starre could not walk down the hall in a straight line with the other children, she wanted to zig-zag from wall to wall.

When she was allowed the freedom to express herself, she shined brighter than the brightest star in the sky; hence her name. Her artwork, writing and acting were the focus of her being. She loved to express herself in a lively way.

In third grade at Cove, an oral report on a famous person was required. The students were to select a famous person, write a report, and reenact a portion of their life, which included donning the garb of that time period. Starre chose the artist, Mary Cassatt. Her presentation was a complete hit!!!

Her classmates were utterly amazed at her unstifled performance, and the teacher sung her praises as well.

Once in middle school, life became a bit more of a challenge as the teenage years progressed. At one point, I was called in to discuss concerns with her learning and comprehension skills or possible lack thereof. Not that her grades were failing but something seemed off cue with her difficulty in taking exams and they couldn't put their finger on it, so they recommended testing. Nothing was found concerning in the results, so we moved forward with Starre being placed in a curriculum designed for those with learning challenges.

Again, she finished that era with another unforgettable execution wielding her newly acquired talents of music and poetry to transform historical facts into a "rap" in place of writing a final report. It was a part of their civil war studies and was entitled "The Battle of Chickamauga." Rest assured her classmates will never forget that battle!

CHAPTER 1

[5:55 a.m. Awakened by the pounding heartbeat, the pulse in my ears, my head on fire, I was impelled to write this down. It's been two years now but the agony that remains seems like yesterday. The salty tears that fall from my eyes down onto my cheeks are melting my soul away. The emptiness is so vast. It feels like a dagger twisting and stabbing a hole in my heart; leaving the raw, red tangled mess inside me open for the judgment and cruelty of society.]1

Come June, we had finally found a shelter to house us. My boyfriend and I were having a little bit of trouble getting along. One day while sitting at a group shelter meeting, Thomas and I were singled out and brought to the office—we were separated into two different rooms. I was feeling very uncomfortable as I wanted to tell the truth knowing the social worker in Massachusetts (MA) had found compassion with that. At the same time, they were asking me too many questions about Thomas and in support of his wishes, I found myself being evasive.

June 5, 2014

Our seven-month-old baby was resting peacefully in his stroller, while we were washing and scrubbing furiously to clean everything up nice. We had just been moved to a new room at the homeless shelter. Unexpectedly, I was

1

called to the office by myself and the social worker had told me that they may need to take Jamez into protective custody.

I went back to our room to await the dreadful answer of Jamez' fate. Jamez melted my heart as he was reaching for me for the first time—it made me feel so loved and needed. The three of us began enjoying this precious family time together. We put Jamez' favorite YouTube song on my computer and I started reading him a book. Our joyful time was abruptly terminated by the social worker, "There is no easy way to say this but we need to take your baby!"

["NO, NO, NOOOO!" I screamed in my heart.

They were stealing my baby but I felt like a criminal. Uncontrollable trembling took over my whole body. I was so frightened. Outwardly, I remained calm and held my tears at bay. I was trying not to frighten Jamez, but I'm sure he was keenly aware something wicked was transgressing. I hugged Jamez tightly. He was grabbing for my earring. I told him to grab whatever he wanted because it may be the last time he would ever touch me.

I held up my arms and surrendered him to their greedy arms like it was nothing, knowing if I resisted it would cause more drama. Then my arms were empty as was my heart, I looked at my hands and wanted to collapse onto the floor. I wanted to yell and cry and kick. Somehow, I kept my dignity because I felt that they would have me committed to a mental health ward if I fell apart like that. I should have been imprisoned for the rage and violent thoughts that were rising inside of me. Taken by the law, robbed without a gun, stolen right from my arms, without a care or thought to the emotional damage it would cause us both; it was like I had been brutally raped! Abducted; a sweet, healthy innocent child cruelly removed from his mother's tenderness. A baby that was loved, crooned and nursed for seven months taken by the Department of Health and Human Services (DHHS), a better acronym would be Destroying Human Hearts and Souls.

When I suddenly became a mother for the first time, my time and my freedom became that of my baby's. The transformation from a single person to a mom is unexplainable. It was a true miracle of the human body; a baby created and nurtured inside my body for nine months was now right here in my arms! Just staring at my little Jamez kept me busy for hours. His presence mesmerized me with intense love that took hold of my whole being. Love so consuming, that I never knew was even possible and it gave me a new feeling of incredible worth. I never wanted to let go. It was difficult to even put my baby Jamez down to sleep. So to lose this precious being that has become my whole life is the single most devastating thing a mother could ever experience. I believe my emotions shut down to protect me.

After leaving the shelter, I walked for what seemed like miles. I wanted to walk off the end of the earth. In a dream-like state, I was beginning to feel the sickness of hell. The pressure was squeezing and strangling my intestines, forcing the bile and heart-wrenching grief upward from deep within. Before I knew it, the inner heat, like hot molten lava, was spewing and spitting from my mouth—erupting like a volcano.

Thomas finally caught up with me, he was fairly calm and gave me hope that we would get our baby back.

Finally acknowledging what had happened, I cried aloud, "My baby, my baby, my baby is gone!" I burst into tears. A mother-child bond severed in two. The blood curdling cry I stifled could only be acknowledged by the souls in heaven; we had no place to go, no place to hide, no home—just the streets. My boyfriend and I held each other all night under a tree, spooning on the bare earth, shivering and crying into each other's hearts, homeless, through cold and rain; no one could understand our agony, all alone frozen in time and space. During that night of eternity, one of my boyfriend's tears fell into my ear. I will never forget that. I think it was then that I subconsciously vowed to harden my heart, to keep that trembling volcano dormant for as long as I existed on this earth.

This kind of suffering is worse than a death. For death can be explained, consoled by others. You can lie in bed and quietly die; crying until no more tears can flow; crying a river or an ocean. So as in time being able to let go, to *forgive God for taking your child. No, this kind of suffering is unforgiveable; a stranger replacing me, stealing my motherhood, hijacking my only reason for living, traumatizing our lives. Keeping the baby's crying a secret, his uncontrollable crying I could hear in my heart. Knowing he wanted his mama back.*

Unable to breathe, unable to walk, unable to speak, I had to draw on my inner strength and rise from my fetal position—open the closet door of death and set my goal to fight. Fight with all I could muster, and follow all their rules and recommendations. Go to all the meetings and counseling all the while my whole reason for living was gone, and the pills I wanted to take were right in my pocket. I didn't know for sure if I could resist from swallowing them.

Somehow, courage evolved from my brokenness. With devastation and despair so complete, only courage could make my life endurable. This is a tragedy of unspeakable magnitude, pain deeper than the valley at Mount Fuji. It has destroyed me like a bolt of lightning— splitting my guts open wide—exposing the charred remains of a life I once had.][2]

---

[2] [*italics*] My rendering through deep empathy and clairsentience of the feelings from my child's soul. *Italics* without brackets are the first person excerpts from Starre's journaling.

4

CHAPTER 2

The day was as hot as an egg sizzling on a fry pan, but not sticky or uncomfortable. The clear sky above was a bright shade of turquois blue. I knew this to be a welcoming factor for boaters. In fact the ocean's surface as I drove by was a million tiny, sparkling diamonds, reflecting sunshine in all directions. In the harbor, there was a school of motor boats and sail boats, enjoying this perfect June day. I arrived at my mom and step-dad's home on Ocean Street, just two houses up from Lothrop Street, which ran along the shore and Dane Street Beach, where I had spent my carefree teenage years growing up. Here on the second floor is where I had planned to have the graduation party for my youngest daughter, Starre Grace. It was the only place large enough for a party and our family was already familiar with the location. Unfortunately, it was a bit awkward for her dad, as he still resided on the first floor, and mind you this had been our family apartment for just over twenty years. Doug and I had divorced three years prior in December of 2005, and he was still very heartbroken and bitter toward me.

My mom (Grammy Gail) is a beautiful woman, she wears her hair naturally gray and stands with a perfect posture. She's a snappy dresser, even in her retirement, and keeps herself busy as a bee. She is devoted to my stepdad, Jack, and they reside on the second floor of a very large three story home, built back at the turn of the century. I went upstairs to prepare what

I could for the party beforehand. I put all the perishable food in the refrigerator and set out the paper goods and decorations. The homemade sheet cake that I had hand decorated was set in the middle of the dining room table as the centerpiece. It was one of my hobbies to decorate cakes and it was frosted in BHS colors of black and orange.

Starre was downstairs getting dressed in her cap and gown. She met us out on the front porch where we traditionally prepared our yearly "first day of school" pictures. We were a bit rushed but Jack and I were able to get a few shots before Starre got picked up for the graduation ceremony. Her long blonde hair hung straight down from the graduation cap. Her face beautiful and proud.

It was there I waited for Starre's older sister, Sunny, to arrive. Sure enough, there she was buzzing around the corner in her little black, Mazda Miata convertible, blonde hair blowing gently in the summer breeze. What a genuine smile that put on my face! Her inner beauty no less shadowed by her outer radiance; she was strikingly adorable and fiercely independent! My first born angel and my first realization of a miracle grown inside me and nurtured with true love. Her birth was amazing as I chose natural childbirth with Doug at my side. I wanted her name to reflect the warmth and power she gave me as I held her to my breast for the very first time. And so it was Sunny Gail, her middle name after her grandmother. She was often a challenge in some ways herself, but my well-learned lessons just became stepping stones for my future.

"Hey Marmaloo!"

Did I tell you I love this girl? Personality to match. We hugged tightly and the two of us hopped into my Pathfinder, Sunny taking shotgun as was her passion to claim. I felt Sunny's essence to be "integrity," as she always remained true to herself and others. She has optimally learned to harness the energy of giving and receiving.

We headed off to Hurd Stadium for the outdoor ceremonies. I had a reserved VIP seating invitation for two. I asked my former husband as first choice to attend with me but he flat out refused, so I asked Sunny. We parked and walked out onto the field where I perused the stadium seating for a roped-off section labeled VIP. I wasn't really sure what it was all about and didn't see anything labeled as such. I asked someone who seemed to be in charge, "Could you tell me where the VIP seating is?" She pointed me right onto the field, just off the stage area to the right.

"Hmph?" I looked at my oldest, and we both shrugged our shoulders in bewilderment. We took our seats, and I opened up the program. There on the very top of the page was our answer!

Invocation Speech

by

Starre Chambers

"Look Sunny," I exclaimed as I pointed out the sweet surprise.

"Wow!" she raised her eyebrows, speechless as I.

Sure enough the class of 2008 was marching down the field toward their seating, directly in front of the stage and to my utter disbelief, my baby girl was marching right up front with the valedictorians! My heart jolted a bit, and I started to tear up. My emotions seldom remained unexpressed.

"She never even told me!"

"You know Starre." Sunny hugged me, always the big sister even to me—a crystal child.

After several introductions by the principal, Mayor and other big wigs, Starre took to the podium. She was never afraid of performing in front of a crowd, it was just part of her nature. Starre was a very attractive petite girl with long, blonde, straight hair falling loosely down her back. She took hold of the microphone, garbed in her black cap and gown with an orange tassel that hung to the right, and began with the introduction.

"Good afternoon everyone—and welcome to the graduation ceremony for the Beverly High School class of 2008!" She began with enthusiasm and got a cheer from the crowd.

"Principal Gallagher, Mayor Scanlon, Dr. Hayes, our Superintendent of School, Mrs. Cessa, Chairperson of the School Committee, as well as other members of the School Committee, members of City Council, Faculty members, parents, family, friends of our Class of 2008 and my fellow classmates:"

Her opening statement followed, "Everyone has just one life to live, but that does not mean we have only one path to follow." I recall thinking how odd this first statement was to me, as we very much believe in everlasting life enriched by *several* lifetimes, each furthering our spiritual growth. Her speech was short but memorable, and applauded with enthusiasm.

Come to find out she had been handpicked for that speech by the principal. She had really worked hard toward the latter part of her senior year, as it was her dream to attend school in California so she could be "discovered" as a little white rapper. Just recently, at the awards ceremony she had received two awards, one for art and one for most improved academically, bringing her grades up to A's from D's and C's. Just goes to show what you can do if you actually apply yourself. She worked super hard to get accepted to Fashion Institute of Design and Merchandising (FIDM) in LA by presenting an amazing portfolio with real pieces of fabric and proving to them that she could indeed complete and comprehend the math requirements.

I still remember the day when she broke the news to me over the phone. I was working my second job at Linens & Things in Reading to support my independence and move to my own apartment in Gloucester after the divorce. I got a call on my cell phone, which I wasn't supposed to answer while on the floor but I picked up anyway when I saw it was Starre.

"Bummy! I got accepted to FIDM! I passed the math requirement! And they loved my portfolio!"

"Oh my God! I am so proud of you! Congratulations! That is so exciting Starre!"

My co-workers shared my joy with the news. It was kind of a "rags to riches" story, as Starre was quite challenged academically, and I never expected her to go to college.

Back on Ocean Street, I got all the food ready with my mom's assistance and amazingly enough, even after the divorce, all of Starre's aunts from her dad's side showed up. I was tickled pink. It was kind of funny, being a Sunday and all, as Sundays were Starre's day of rest. And to my chagrin, sure enough, she planted herself on the couch in the living room with her diploma and didn't much move!!!! It was kind of a kick in the ass, after all my preparations, but that was my angel.

We had a very busy summer that was spent mostly in Gloucester with me. We had college matters to attend to. At one point, we were contacted for a down payment to the apartment where Starre would be taking residence while attending school. They wanted $3000.00! "Eeek," that was *not* in my budget.

"Starre, look, I mean, I do not have three thousand dollars to put down for housing."

After a moment of intensity, "Well, I do. I have money in my bedroom."

Are you kidding! Somehow my little enigma, who was always hitting me up for money, had secretly squirreled away that much money in her bedroom!!! She had been working at Dairy Queen, and I had continued to give her $20.00 per week for cleaning the bathroom even after I had moved out.

Starre also worked on some creative projects for an American Miss Pageant. She designed her own formal dress with pink and baby blue dye; her two favorite colors adding sequins and lacing up the back, which was cut apart and restitched from a gown a friend had given her. She perfected a talent show project and choreographed a rap dance and song with an uplifting message to young girls and their self-esteem. As usual, her acting talents were acknowledged with applause and she won the 1st runner-up talent award. She was truly amazing in my eyes, the only one who had the whole crowd roaring with laughter as she performed her "Pantene" skit. I believe she really should have gotten first place but her "homey" style was not quite in the proper fashion etiquette for a beauty pageant winner, so they gave her the runner-up award, which was well received. If they had an award for creativity, she definitely would have gotten first place!

CHAPTER 3

When you endlessly face the wind
It hardens not just your face
But your soul as well"

At the end of August, Doug drove Starre and myself to Logan Airport for the trip to California. I wanted to be sure Starre got situated in her dorm at the LA campus of FIDM. The flight was non-stop and pleasant enough, sunny the whole way, which made for pretty views out the window.

"Look at the clouds Bummy, they look like a field of cotton balls. I feel like I could jump out the window and play in the softness like the "Care Bears"—rolling around and sliding down rainbows!"

We both giggled aloud, her mind was so exotic. I thoroughly enjoyed her imagination.

From LAX, we caught a cab to the dorm which was off-site from the main campus. I gave the cab driver the address, we checked in at the gate, and he delivered us to the apartment complex. This was luxury living. We had driven past the club house and the pool on the way. The walls were covered in fresh white paint, and the floors adorned wall to wall with a shaggy carpet. It had central air, was clean, modern and WiFi was included. The kitchen had stainless steel appliances, a garbage disposal and lots of

11

cabinet space. A table bar with stools separated the living room which came equipped with a wall-mounted 42" TV screen. There were two double bedrooms, so three roommates. Starre briefly met the other girls as everyone was entirely consumed with unpacking.

While Starre unpacked, I read through the school agenda. There was an orientation/luncheon meeting at the club house. We were famished, so off we went. My young adventurer was already feeling a little uncomfortable as the other girls wanted to go to the pool. That was not Starre's thing. She wasn't into TV either. After we ate, we listened to a couple speakers and mingled a little before leaving. It was really awkward, even for me.

We headed back to the apartment to take inventory of the things we would need to buy. We looked up where the nearest Linens & Things was located so that I could take advantage of my 20 percent discount. We caught a bus that delivered us to a shopping plaza where Linens & Things was located. After grabbing a carriage, we floated about the store. We finally found suitable bedding as Starre was very precise with her style and color requirements. The kitchen accessories were next.

We wheeled the loaded up, the over-the-top shopping cart outside. The view of the mountains in the distance with the iconic palm trees in the foreground was like eye candy to us, not the typical backdrop we were used to seeing in Beverly, MA.

I called a cab three times but they never showed up. It seemed that we were in a different location than we thought, I had been sending a cab to the wrong city! About an hour later, we finally got picked up. The traffic was excruciating, and we didn't get back to the apartment until dark.

One of Starre's roommates offered to give me a ride back to my hotel. She had GPS but that did not eliminate the horrific traffic jam near the Hollywood Bowl. I felt badly for the inconvenience, gave her money for gas, knowing full well that it didn't make up for her time.

The next day I met up with Starre for some lunch, we bought a few groceries, and went back to the apartment. She really seemed distant around the other girls. I could tell she just wasn't fitting in, and it concerned me. I tried my best to make sure she was acclimated and had what she needed—there was no turning back now. I went through the schedule of upcoming events with her that were planned before classes commenced.

Once on the plane, my eyes began to fill up with tears, so I kept my gaze toward the window. I felt so nervous about leaving Starre Grace in such a far-away place all alone. The lady who sat next to me must have sensed my apprehension.

"If you need to get up to stretch or go to the bathroom, just tap me. I don't mind at all."

Her words did comfort me. I settled in for the five-hour flight home, mesmerized in a surreal kind of way.

The first few days were a huge adjustment for Starre. There wasn't even a food plan included in the tuition—"ugh," things had really changed since I attended college. I remember her calling for some direction just a couple days later. She had missed an important orientation and was in tears. She was very uncomfortable with her roommates and had to venture out on her own to find the way to the school as the "dorm" was quite far from the campus. I think we were both terrified.

One night, she called me from outside the dorm while the other three girls and some friends were inside. They had made fun of her, and I could feel her loneliness so deeply. I understood her longing and her desire to find some tranquility through nature, like we had raised her in. I felt so much empathy for her, I knew she didn't have enough life experiences or common sense in some areas to adjust quite readily to a large urban city situation so far away from home. And she just wasn't like those "valley girls." Her chosen footwear was boots! She didn't wear bathing suits or shorts! She didn't like to shave either, as she thought the hair was better soft rather than prickly. She just wasn't a girly-girl city girl at all. She definitely had some very rough days. But she made the best of it, found her way

13

around, began to hang with some rapper buddies, and just concentrated on her school work.

I was able to fly her back home for her first Christmas. She was quite responsible in catching her plane and moving through the layover in Texas. She arrived in Boston on time. I drove into the city by myself and parked across the street in a parking garage, as Logan airport did not allow idling cars at the arrival area since the September 11, 2001 terrorist attack.

When I saw her, I screamed with delight and ran to meet her. It had only been three months but I missed her dearly. We hugged, and I stepped back to take a good look at her before we went back to the car. She was so cute, her creativity was expressed in her everyday outfits.

Christmas felt somewhat awkward for Starre because I was living by myself in Gloucester, and her dad was still in Beverly with her brother Sam. Sunny, her big sister, lived in Salem with a roommate. Little miss congeniality managed to enjoy the holidays despite the separation, but not without a bit of a guilt trip on me regarding the "vows" of marriage.

It was the return flight that caused some discourse. I had read the arrival time as the departure time, "ugh." When I realized my mistake it was too late to fix it. Starre completely fell apart, crying and screaming— which was a complete switch. It was usually me that was the emotional drama queen, I had left that part of me back on Ocean Street. I called the airport to find out what to do.

"You will have to be on stand-by, so you need to just come."

I thought it would have been easier to book us the flight first, but anyway, I guess that's just the way it works. When we got there, Starre was rebooked on a flight the next morning. We had to spend the night at the airport. I stayed with her since it was my mistake. It was an awful night, and we definitely did not sleep a wink. Once she was in the TSA line, I kissed her goodbye as I had to go straight to work.

By the third semester, Starre had found her own place to live. I spoke with her landlady by phone, and we faxed forms back and forth until everything was in order. Starre had gone through hell, trying to move all her stuff by herself. She expressed her agony of trip after trip of lugging stuff on and off the bus. Finally, Starre had some peace of mind.

This was when she stated dating Eloe, a fellow musician from the UK.

CHAPTER 4

I wanted more than anything to find the man I would be with forever. In California, while attending FIDM I met Eloe. When our infatuation started, I told him I had traveled across the United States just to meet him. He was from Amsterdam, Holland. He was a cocky type of guy, filled with pride and very stubborn. He also had a sensitive side. He made me feel a way no other man ever had. One day he told me that he didn't like to see me cry. Even though he was not controlling about it, I took those words to heart as I just wanted to make him happy.

When I was alone, I found myself crying in the mirror and hearing his voice in my head. Smiling through tears, I cried harder. Smiling hurt because I was trying to be something I was not.

Eloe was in the studio, making music most nights until about 3 a.m. One night he invited me to go to the studio with him, I declined due to it being my "relaxation day." He never invited me again. This made me wonder what went on during those sessions and found myself having anxiety around him going. I became very jealous, I was insecure and I acted out. My tantrums ignited his temper and so our relationship was kind of drama-filled.

After a while, I started feeling happy when he was not around, but for some reason I could not act on breaking up with him.

A short while after her move to the new apartment, I had bought bus tickets for Starre and Eloe to meet my boyfriend Joe and myself out in San Diego while we were on vacation. The day did not start out too well for Starre, as Eloe must have been in dreamland and would not wake up. After banging on his door and screaming, Starre had to go it alone and ended up missing the bus. Rebooked on a later bus, she arrived two hours later, I knew Joe was a little pissed but he wasn't one to say much. We got some lunch and drove to the San Diego Zoo.

It was a beautiful, clear sunny day as it almost always seems to be in the lower part of California. The plan had been to get to the zoo early, so we could get in line at the panda cage. The late start didn't allow for this, but we got a few glances of the playful black and white bears through the glass even though our view was obstructed by all the moving people in line. Zoos are one of my favorite things to do, an escape from the often harsh realities of life. We took lots of pictures, but got really tired out due to the heat. We found ourselves scrambling to see all the exhibits.

Joe and I decided to drive Starre back to LA rather than stick her on a bus again as it was easy to reroute a bit in order to accommodate. It was getting late and it was a much longer drive than Joe had thought. He was exhausted and was definitely getting frustrated. Starre wanted to pick up some of her things from Eloe's because she had the ride. Eloe had helped gather some of Starre's things from her old apartment and was storing them at his place. I helped her make several trips back and forth with the boxes, and then I got to see her new apartment. What a step down from the luxury apartments at FIDM. It was basically in a slum area called Korea town. It didn't matter to Starre, it was home and she was delighted with it. It even had a "tub!"

After Eloe and I had been together for about a year, I became pregnant. I always "trusted in God" that when I found the right man, I would become pregnant. I never used any form of birth control. I was excited; I planned in my mind how I would finish school and such. Telling many people, the last to break the news to was my mother and I was scared. When I told my mother, she expressed worry and told me that I wouldn't be able to see my dreams flourish if I continued my pregnancy. My mother believed I was not ready to be a mom, she actually confessed that she had been through the exact same thing when she was in college. I was nineteen and I envisioned my experience as a mother in a happy relationship that would give our child a good foundation. I knew that Eloe's and my relationship was not the best and so I considered my mom's advice and steered toward the abortion.

The day I was scheduled to go into the clinic, Eloe asked me to wait one more day. I told him, "I can't." I was eight weeks at that time and I was led to believe that the baby did not have a heartbeat. I knew if I waited it would be too late. We walked to the clinic together. When I went in, they did an internal ultrasound and I believe I started screaming. I am sensitive to doctors doing internal exams. A female nurse came in to make sure everything was okay. They told me I did not have to do this and I told them it was not about the abortion, it was about the invasiveness. When I went into the procedure room, I met the male doctor who would be doing the procedure. He made some type of joke with me that I did not find very funny. I was disgusted that this male did abortions for a living, and so I asked if the nurse would be present for the whole procedure. The nurse assured me she would be present and they put a mask on me that put me under. I woke up tossing and turning and noticed my left breast was showing out of my hospital gown and quickly covered it up. They had me take some Ibuprophen before leaving.

In a daze, I walked into the doorway of the waiting room to be greeted by Eloe. He helped me walk and called a taxi. He bought us some lunch on the way home. When we got to my apartment in Korea town, Eloe passed out. I just sat there. I decided to go to the store and even though I had been told not to lift anything heavy, I came back with a bunch of groceries. I wasn't as scarred about the abortion as I was thinking about that doctor—I was so disgusted with him, I mean he was just a sicko in my mind.

19

Knowing Starre's relationship with Eloe was extremely tumultuous, I had tried to intervene a couple of times. I spoke with him on the phone, asking him to be more respectful, knowing full well that Starre was just as disrespectful to him as her painful insecurities had begun to change her temperament. The news of her pregnancy really made me worry about Starre's emotional well-being. I was glad Eloe could be there for her. Looking back, I don't know why I *ever* gave her that advice, it's just not right; I can only pray for God's forgiveness toward our ignorance. I knew in my heart that this was the turning point in her life. She did love him but I was aware that she felt empty and betrayed. Eloe's mom, Lynn flew in to visit a few times. Lynn treated Starre with a lot of respect and kindness. She filled in as a "mom" when she was in LA. If it weren't for Lynn, Starre's twentieth birthday would have been spent alone. Lynn took her and her son out to celebrate. I actually got to talk with Lynn that evening and thanked her with all my heart. She seemed like a sweetheart to me and I knew she was just that to Starre.

After three years and many attempts to leave Eloe, I finally stood my ground and he left. After a while, I tried to contact him but he would never respond. Now it seemed he was standing his ground. I loved Eloe and wanted to accept the things I did not like. I remember him telling me that a relationship sticks through thick and thin, but I guess it was just too late.

I became deeply depressed, and felt I needed to be with someone new. I tried talking with men on OkCupid. I adopted a stray cat from the neighborhood that had been neglected and abused. Thinking she should have some "tough" name, I thought about naming her Scruffy or something like that but after getting to know her, I named her Buggy. She had a clingy affectionate personality with a twist, probably due to trust issues. Additionally, I got a white dove I named Serene.

CHAPTER 5

At some point, my Starre was finally able to hook up with a woman named Karen. Karen had been a good friend of one of Starre's aunts back here on the east coast, but had moved to the west coast after high school. So it seemed like a good plan to have Starre meet her while in California as she could step in as another role model. Karen was married and had two young girls. They lived in Winnetka, which was about an hour away from LA. She really stepped in as a positive support to Starre for a short period of time. Starre was even hired to baby sit her daughters and was paid quite well.

Despite all the trials and tribulations, in June of 2010 my baby girl graduated! I admired her for sticking it out and finishing school. Her dad having softened his heart a little toward me agreed accompany me to fly out to LA so we could attend the graduation at the Staples Center! Another momentous event!

The morning of the graduation, I recall it being crazy at the train station due to the Lakers' parade. There were security officers holding back all the purple and gold dressed fans.

It was funny because Doug and I were sitting high up in the bleachers watching the FIDM graduates below, and we could see remnants of confetti left over from the Laker's big championship win the evening before. We ended up taking our graduate and a couple of her friends—fellow rappers out to lunch at California Pizza Kitchen. We had so much fun; another memory secured in time. We were very proud of Starre. Doug and I stayed at our daughter's digs for the week.

It was a comfort to know that we could go almost anywhere in California via public transportation. Doug and I got to meet Karen and the girls. Karen hosted a delicious salmon dinner for us with salad and pasta, and dessert. Her home was a one level modern ranch and quite posh. We sat out back on the patio until the sun went down. The crescent moon was like a saucer holding back the rain according to Doug's philosophy. The west coast has its perks, and we actually got to pick a couple of grapefruits from a tree right in their backyard. The citrus fragrance filled our senses with euphoria and rubbed onto our hands with freshness.

Our last day together, we rented a car and drove to a redwood grove in a northern part of California. It was a pleasure to get out of the city, and we were overjoyed with the scenery along the way. When we entered the park, the sweet smell of pine engaged our sense of smell, and our hearts filled up with gratitude; truly in our glory to be witness to this master-piece of God's creation. Being a nature loving family at heart, we knew a place like this would not be easily forgotten. Spending time outdoors in nature raises the spirit and solidifies a reverence for mother earth. Starre still loved to pose, and she was wearing a yellow velour jogging suit. The contrast of the brilliant yellow against the earthy tones of brown and green made for some truly amazing pictures. There was a pathway that led us through the ancient forest. The mossy landscape cushioned our feet while the picturesque scenery felt surreal; trees so tall we couldn't see the tops. The woods were darkened while only streaks of sunshine poured down through the thick tree cover. Tranquility washed over us like a blanket; so in our element to be hiking in the woodlands yet so unlike *anything* we had ever experienced before. Standing inside trees and realizing how old they were truly took our breath away. The day was so peaceful, even the ride back remains etched into our minds as we drove into the sunset spotting the silhouette of a bison up on a hill.

My young graduate ended up landing a part-time job at a sock factory called K. Bell. She was a little office worker! She was hoping to score a job in the music industry as well. She had been collaborating with rappers, performing shows and doing her own videos which piqued her interest in that area. Interviews were hard to schedule, the fashion jobs were quite competitive, and getting there via public transportation was actually quite a task. Even K. Bell was an hour and a half away.

One day an old friend from Beverly was out there on a business trip, so he looked up Starre and took her out to eat—big time. Lobster and steamers! In their conversation, Starre had mentioned that she was looking into a position in the music industry, so he generously took her shopping for a new outfit including shoes!

Some days were better than others, at some point, bedbugs had come into the picture! Her apartment was infested. The landlord had fumigated a couple times but it was really hard with the pets. It was a harrowing experience that seemed to get worse when she had an alcoholic friend stay with her. My poor baby girl endured red, itchy rashes and felt secretly isolated from society, not wanting anyone to know. When Karen discovered this, she was impelled to ditch her relationship with my Starre, unable to take the risk of bedbug infestation.

Meanwhile, my ambitious daughter enrolled at The Musician's Institute and took a course called *Independent artist program* which was about music recording and managing. The course required an Apple laptop, and she was able to find a used one through eBay. I was really quite proud of her—working part time and continuing her education as well.

CHAPTER 6

I had been talking with my friend Jason from MA about being my music manager. He and I were excited to try and make that work. Jason had just been laid off from a job he hated and was on the verge of running out of his unemployment money, so I told him to come out to LA. After scheduling him to arrive in time to "pet-sit," I was off to MA. I had met a seemingly loyal and respectful dude named Roe on OkCupid. He was from Tennessee, his profile excited me as we had a 99 percent match rate. After talking with him for a few months, I thought I was falling in love with him. We had arranged to meet. My family had prepared for me to visit home for a week, and I thought it would be the opportune time to meet Roe. I bought a plane ticket for him and scheduled him to arrive shortly after me, so my family could be there to ensure my safety.

My mom and sister Sunny met me at the Manchester Airport in New Hampshire. It's a less hectic airport than Boston. We ate some lunch in the car and waited for Roe to arrive. We had a really awesome week. Roe met my grandparents, and we did some hiking and a lot of visiting. My mom and sister both loved Roe. They found him to be engaging, respectful, polite, and appreciative, important virtues that were absent from any of my past boyfriends. At the week's end, Roe and I had a sad departure as we flew out to our separate states.

Meanwhile back in LA, I had other problems. Things with Jason had started out so great—he had dinner ready for me when I got home from work and was keeping the apartment picked up, but things rapidly deteriorated. Before long, I was coming home to Jason drinking vodka mixes and realized he was a serious alcoholic. To make matters worse, Jason had a secret crush on me and was very jealous that I was always talking to Roe. He was also jealous of my friends. One night he even had an episode in front of one of my friends losing his temper.

After bearing it enough, I called the cops on him. Maybe five or more policemen came. A woman officer stayed outside of my door with me and they had to use a Taser on Jason in order for him to cooperate. I'm so sensitive; I was ashamed that my pets were witnessing this.

The worst part was, when I got home from work the next day there he was sitting on my porch! He tried to make me feel guilty for "evicting" him. While I was able to eventually get him out of my home completely, Jason has never forgiven me. Making up his side of the story to comfort himself; in his mind, I took him away from everything he knew, got him arrested, beaten by the cops, and then threw him out on the street.

To return to my "Roe-man-ce," I was eager for us to experience our physical relationship, and I bought Roe a plane ticket again, this time to visit me in California. The problems that arose caused havoc with our relationship. First off, I was working full-time and found it hard to keep my apartment neat and clean which was a huge unsettling factor for Roe—he was neat to the point of military training; he even ironed his own clothes. I had let it go too long and found it overwhelming on where to even begin. What's more were the bedbugs! The colonies had started to wind down about the time Jason had come to live with me. The fierce little biters became rampant again—in part because bedbugs love to feed on blood with high alcohol content. Yes, the landlord knew and had treated, but nothing worked. I let Roe know before he came, but he couldn't even imagine that I was as serious as I was. I think he assumed I was exaggerating.

Things were really stressful for Roe, he couldn't stay in my house. I hated not being home for my pets, while we slept on rooftops and in stairwells. During the day, Roe hung out with my friend Mario, but he missed the one-on-one time we had experienced in MA. Eventually, he went home and did not talk with me like he used to. I was once again heartbroken.

CHAPTER 7

My forlorn daughter had finally found a new apartment in another section of LA. It seemed to be in a somewhat better section of the city and had a gated entrance. She moved all her stuff bus by bus, laborious trip by laborious trip. It was an immense task for a single girl to accomplish, but her "I can do it" attitude got it done. She had dried all her linens and clothing on high heat at a laundromat, hoping to kill all the bed bugs. When she moved in she kept her clothes in tall plastic bags in the large open living room just to be sure. Little did she know, that she would soon encounter another horror—roaches! Another truly repulsive consequence to inner city living. When she got home in the evenings there were hundreds of roaches all over the kitchen walls and floor—no exaggeration!

Soon another romance resulted from Okcupid. This boy's name was Carl. He flew in from Ohio and next thing I knew Starre was telling me that she was engaged!!!!!!

"What!" This I just couldn't believe. After her last two experiences? It just didn't make any sense. I was able to visit in April of 2011 for her birthday. We went shopping, and I bought her a bunch of stuff to decorate her new home. It was quite a chore getting it all back to the apartment by bus. It made me really appreciate what she had gone through on her last two moves.

I loved the new apartment. It was quite spacious and had 14-foot high ceilings. The walls were all white. Oversized windows allowed abundant sunshine and fresh air to enter. The living room had wall to wall deep green carpet. The bathroom was decorated with lime green and turquoise. Quite pretty after I scrubbed and put up the new towels and scatter rugs. She had an open closet between the living room and the bathroom. It was here she kept her newly acquired fish tank with nine fish.

I took my 21-year-old birthday girl and her "fiancé" out to dinner. It was an upscale restaurant just behind the Staples Center. We enjoyed our seafood dinner and sang "happy birthday" when the waiter brought out cake. It was dusk when we got outside. That magical time between day and night. We playfully posed with the statues and snapped some fun pictures. It was when we got back to the apartment that I realized the enormous roach problem! I quickly understood that my sweet angel had gone from the frying pan right into the fire!

I found out that my daughter had lost her job in December. She was hanging on financially at that point. Having tried a job at a fast food counter, her feet suffered and she started having bunion issues and had to quit.

I questioned Carl about his intentions of marrying my daughter, and he seemed pretty sure. I could tell that Starre was a bit apprehensive of the idea. I guess she didn't know how to say, "No."

I stayed for five days and we also visited the Griffith Observatory in southern California. I got to see Carl in action—he was super devoted in a "puppy dog" sort of way. Starre, being true to her nature stopped often to pose taking advantage of his overly eager personality to take pictures of her. It was actually sickening to me, and I was getting impatient. The observatory is a really great place to visit, we had experienced it with her dad in the evening during our stay in June of 2010, so visiting during the daylight was a whole new learning experience. Anyway, Carl ended up being more of a lug than a boyfriend/fiancée, so he soon enough packed up and moved back home.

Carl and I met on OkCupid. We started out having dreamy video chats and he always responded immediately to me, giving me plenty of attention. I brought him out to LA, and he moved into the new apartment with me. The infestation of roaches did not come between our love. Carl and I shared the passion of music. Making songs and music videos together, we also collaborated with my other artist friends in LA. His attentiveness fed my ego, but left me suspicious; there just seemed to be something off balance with him. Ever since dating Eloe, I had trouble being in love with men who were too sweet.

CHAPTER 8

By June 2012, my baby girl finally gave up and came home to live in Georgetown, MA with her sister Sunny and myself. My amazing Sunny is a creator of dreams, anything she sets her mind to will most surely be manifested by Godspeed and soon enough become her reality. She bought her own home in June of 2010 and while by no means financially rich, she is definitely financially abundant! It made me wonder if Miss Starre had taken a pause in life as she seemed to be temporarily losing this amazing ability in herself. If I were to guess, I believed her insecurities had grown to haunt her, but like I have always believed when we fall from grace, "It's just one step backwards before we take two steps forward."

The pickup in Boston was a complete nightmare. She had missed her plane! Her pets were already shipped—a cat and some fish. She was able to take the dove on the plane with her. Starre has a way to disrupt everyone around her while remaining calm inside. An enigma, when she is grounded and focused, I believe her essence to be true "patience."

I had a heck of a time trying to find out where to pick the pets up. I'm not all that good with direction as it is and going into Boston by myself can launch my anxiety. Starre had called crying, she told me they were going to send the animals to a shelter if I didn't pick them up by noon. When I had finally found the cargo area and got Buggy out to my car, she was a complete wreck. In the car, I let her out of the cage to pet her. Her stress caused her to shed profusely. There were white cat hairs all over the interior of my car. The fish were safe in a large Styrofoam cooler. I succeeded in getting them safely back to Georgetown and awaited the rescheduled flight information from Starre.

Back in Boston, I picked up my long lost wanderer, who had tried her best at a new life of fame only to be sorely disappointed. We ended up setting up a tent in the driveway. Sunny's house was not really big enough for another guest and her dogs were not too thrilled to share their home with a cat.

I began a music business website once back in MA. It enabled me to utilize my talents to assist other artists while simultaneously helping myself. I named my company I.Q. Productionz, standing for inner quality. I offered graphic design, recording/mastering, writing skills, photography/video service, dancers, and promotion. Promotion included websites, news articles, booking shows, and social media marketing. Carl helped out with mastering and social media marketing. He also had the opportunity to record local artists in Cleveland, while I recorded local artists in Georgetown.

Starre and Buggy stayed in the tent until the snow began to fall. We moved her into the living room which luckily was enclosed with a sliding glass door, so it physically separated the cat from the dogs. That did not keep Ollie, the big dog from barking like crazy and jumping at the door when Buggy decided to show herself. It was kind of a nuisance for Sunny as the living room was the direct route to the backyard, and now she had to lead the dogs around from the front door.

Starre found a job in Beverly working on website development. She was able to ride into work with myself. She also had a small online business venture. Although nothing was very financially lucrative.

Soon she met another boy from Ohio named Thomas. She spent hours on the phone talking with him. She felt that he had the same spiritual beliefs as herself and that he was a "twin flame."

Carl had inadvertently introduced me to Thomas. I was told he was a music manager who could help run the Cleveland branch of I.Q. Productionz. We played phone tag a few times before being able to talk one-on-one. When I listened to his voicemails, I thought he sounded like a "fake" professional; he stumbled on his words here and there and had a voice that reminded me of a guy whom I had met in LA that I thought was a creep. (Ha, first red flag!) The day we first talked, he told me he had watched my music videos, and that I reminded him of himself. In my mind, I was saying "yah, yah, yah, you ain't turning me on to you—nice try."

The next morning after speaking with the "music manager," Thomas, I felt connected to him somehow. I had this feeling take over my body, and I texted him something conveying this, like maybe he experienced it too. After that we started talking more romantically and were drawn to each other in our dreams.

I needed to see him. Thinking of how, I thought maybe I could pawn my gold jewelry for a plane ticket. My dad didn't want me to do that so he bought a plane ticket for me. The passion inside me was so strong for Thomas. I had butterflies in my stomach the whole plane ride. When I got to the Cleveland airport, I called Thomas. I don't even think he picked up right away! When I got a hold of him, I was upset that he was not waiting for me at the airport; he said he was on his way. When he finally got there, he tried to kiss me and I turned my head. Approaching his car, I was disgusted that it was so dirty and shabby looking. What's worse was that Thomas told me he did not smoke weed and the car smelled like it. His excuse was that it was not really his car. Once at his house, I was again stunned that it was so grungy—my perception of Thomas was becoming tarnished. When getting closer to Thomas, I smelled that the weed stench was actually on his breath.

Right there and then I had all the answers. Thomas was not committed or truthful. Despite my observations and all the "red flags," I held on to my passion and took an unwise chance that ended up putting me through an emotional rollercoaster, which I have endured like a true soldier.

Despite the warnings, quite naturally I let myself fall in love with Thomas. (Starre's Grammy Gail used to say, "Good things come to those who wait.") When the week was up for me to return home, I remembered departing Roe; I did not want to do that again. I asked and bartered with my sister to let Thomas stay with us and she agreed. Thomas called one of his friends to buy him a plane ticket, and we booked his trip the night before my departure. We were even able to get on the same flight.

Once in Georgetown, I realized Thomas was not happy. Our love was not as important to him as business. My friend, Marshall, whom I was working for owned a studio in Beverly. Marshall had given Thomas the notion that working in his studio would be likely. Thomas was upset that I was not nagging Marshall about his interview. He just didn't have any patience and was unable to understand my tactics or Marshall's current commitments. Ironically after Thomas left, which was the day after Valentine's Day, Marshall texted me asking if he could meet with him.

Again, heartbreak took its toll. I cried and blew my nose so often that the floor was like walking on a bed of squishy marshmallows. Even my sister came in to comfort me and hugged me while I laid in bed, bawling my eyes out.

When I was done feeling sorry for myself, I knew it would be wise to do something to pep myself back up. My friend Amelia asked me to stay with her for a week in a nearby town. I was able to bring my pets along as well. Surprisingly things were not much better there. I was still depressed, and Amelia and I got in minor quarrels that left the air stale and distant. I believe Amelia decided to buy me a pregnancy test. It was either that or I had gotten it before I went to visit. Either way, I was filled with a cocktail of emotions when the result was positive.

CHAPTER 9

By February, Starre Grace announced her pregnancy. In my heart, I knew she just wasn't mature enough to take care of a baby. While Sunny did not particularly like Thomas, she felt that together she and Starre would be able to work it out. She also knew the emotional trauma of any alternative. To be fair it's not that Sunny didn't like Thomas, it's just that she saw right through him. She knew right from the beginning that something was "off" with him. I, on the other hand, was taken in just like Starre. He was a handsome dude and had a genuine smile that was very warming. His face was perfectly symmetrical, with a dark moustache and a tightly trimmed beard that just accentuated his jaw line. His hair was curly but also kept short. Even though he seemed a bit insecure, I was curious to know more about him. When allowed to express himself, he did carry on a bit. I could see that he had the charisma to talk a starving dog off a meat wagon, and he would do so if you let your guard down.

To quote Thomas' grandmother, Bonnie, "Grown folk are gonna do what grown folk are gonna do." Miss independent was "grown folk" now, and she chose to keep the baby. The next thing we knew, the pregnant mama had decided to move out to Ohio with Thomas taking residence at his great grandma, Mavie's home. From what I understand, she had raised him as a child. She was somewhat frail, quite spry for her age. Starre kept in touch by phone, texting, and emails. We adapted to the idea of her pregnancy and enjoyed the pictures she sent us. It became obvious that she loved being pregnant. And even though we didn't have a lot of contact, the pictures of her growing baby bump were shown with tenderness and outward joy. Unfortunately, her private nature caused her to remain uncomfortable in Ohio. She told me that she always felt like Mavie was spying on her, which I was sure was not her intent. The rest of Thomas' family used to visit on the weekends, and Starre wasn't comfortable with them either.

I had decided to throw her a baby shower as our anticipation of a baby grew in happy bounds. The mom-to-be and her odd baby-daddy caught a bus back to MA for the event. At this point, I was living in Salem with Joe, with my soon to be husband. Joe was my second romantic love and a quiet soul. He was somewhat short in stature but he was tall with virtue and very Italian! Most of the time, he would have a cigar hanging off his lips. We had a tiny home that we rented, but it had a small extra bedroom in which we let Starre and Thomas stay in.

The shower was very successful. We were blessed with a bright September day full of sunshine. Four or five of Starre's high school girl-friends were able to attend. A couple of my friends, my mom, Sunny, and Joe's two sisters joined in the celebration as well. Everyone thought the food was marvelous. We had decorated a chair in the corner by the windows and sunshine flooded the living room with joy. There were so many gifts and a huge bag of clothes from Sam's girlfriend! We played some fun shower games; everything went on as planned.

A few days later, Joe ended up finding out some disturbing stuff about Thomas' past and to my horror kicked him out, effective immediately. Take note that Joe had told me Thomas was not welcome in our house at all—ever again, I think I was so overwhelmed with emotion for Starre that I didn't hear that final request. My Joe said he was a thief and he didn't trust him and when Joe made up his mind, that was it—he was very stubborn. Of course, Joe said Starre could stay but quite obviously, she wanted to be with Thomas. I drove Starre and Thomas to her dad's where he was living at one of his sister's and had to just drop her off. They weren't able to get in touch with Doug. I drove off in tears as I had just left my very pregnant daughter on the side of the road at her aunt's house. This was not the kind of life I wanted for a daughter of mine. I knew Joe may have thought he was just sticking up for me, but sometimes I look back and wonder how I let that whole scene unfold. It was unnatural for a man to come in between a mother–daughter bond like that—almost unforgivable—he's lucky I love him as I do.

The unwelcome pair rented a car and drove back to Ohio leaving behind all the shower gifts in our living room, much to Joe's dismay. Joe and I both dislike clutter, although I can better deal with it especially when I know it's temporary.

While in Ohio my pregnancy was progressing uneventfully. Thomas and I tried to start a business and were unsuccessful. Around six months into my pregnancy, I was arrested! Thomas had thought of a grand scheme to pass a bad check and get a car and I fell for it. [I have to interject a thought here—I have a feeling that both parties had told their respective families that it was their mates' idea when they were **both** liable parties to the crime.] *He was also incarcerated. I was so depressed. The detective told me that Thomas said that he had just met me. I was horrified--it made me feel unwanted and ashamed. My pets were left at Thomas' great grandmas' and she wasn't even home to care for them, nor did I have anyone's phone number to make arrangements. First, we were put into a holding cell, and I wore all orange. Then we were transferred to the Cuyahoga County Jail. Oddly enough, we rode together handcuffed. Thomas looked so sorry. He told me he loved me and urged the officers to play peaceful music for the baby. After a week, my dad, with the help of my mom was able to put up the money to bail me out.*

Upon being freed, I got out of jail with no money, no makeup, and in a city I did not know well. However, I found a train station, showed them some papers and they gave me a free pass to get back to where we were staying. When I arrived at the house, I saw one of Thomas' aunts and told her my story. Later that night Thomas' grandmother Bonnie showed up. She felt that I should go home and leave Thomas! [Bonnie and her family were extremely disturbed that Thomas and Starre had been engaged in illegal acts in their mother's home. Mavie was so frightened after the police had gone and searched the house that she was afraid to stay there.] *Bonnie was concerned about our relationship and expressed that I would be better off going home as she did not think that Thomas could ever be what I wanted. I told her I did not want to go, that I wanted to be with Thomas. Bonnie told me I could stay if I helped take of her mother and that's what I did.* [Bonnie had told me that all she had asked Starre to do was wake her mother up in the morning and get her something to eat for breakfast.]

A couple of months passed as Thomas and I exchanged letters. One letter Thomas sent was his hands traced so that he could touch my belly. I was still very depressed because we were separated. It seemed like forever, but I knew that Thomas' family wanted to be sure he [learned his lesson] before they bailed him out.

When labor started my girl was on the phone keeping me informed of the progress. The midwife who was delivering the baby kept telling Starre to wait at home due to her request to have a drug-free labor. I was getting a little scared myself, I thought she should be at the hospital where she would be safe if the labor was to progress more quickly than expected. I ended up going to bed.

Contractions had been slow but steady most of the evening. I did all my last minute prepping for the hospital. I was very sensitive and irritable. At one point, Thomas' great grandma was laughing at me, and I snapped back at her. It was getting late about 12:00 a.m. on the 27th of October, and after calling the midwives again, the lady on call told me not to come in since I wanted low intervention. She did not believe I was in labor and warned me that they would have to run tests if I showed up. I knew my contractions were a minute apart, despite my pain I was able to count to 60 between them. I told Thomas to call his mother for a ride since the hospital was about an hour away. He called her, however, he decided to dilly-dally and take a shower so we waited on him when his mother arrived. I had all types of things packed to go. From a little basket for my son to sleep in, clothes and diapers to electric candles, crystals, and a humidifier.

When we got to the hospital, the nurse checked my cervix. She found that I was 9 cm dilated. During the process, she actually popped my water and I began to cry. She looked at me with confusion and wondered why I was crying. No, it wasn't painful, it was emotional, and I felt abused in a way; like she popped it before it was time.

I guess the nurse just thought the baby should come soon and after she massaged my birth canal opening, she urged me to push. I had read lots of books on birth, and I knew I was told to trust my body but it was my first birth. I wanted to be sure it was going to go right and of course, I was vulnerable. The midwife was called in, and they just kept telling me to push, and I began to get very angry.

They want to see me push, they can't tell that I am pushing? I'll show them, *I thought. I pushed as hard as I could, my face beet red and the nurses and Thomas pushed my legs back. I felt a burning at the opening of my birth canal, but was so angry I pushed through it and soon enough little Jamez came to meet us! It was said that he stuck his hand out first, exposing the sign language "I love you." From there I began breastfeeding Jamez, and Thomas and I became physical parents.*

<"Hi Mommy. Thank you for taking such good care of me while I was in your womb. I know you fed me with healthy food and did not do any drugs or drink alcohol. Remember, we made a promise to each other before we left heaven. My purpose is a difficult one. I am going to melt your heart with love, and then I am going to hurt you more deeply than you can even

imagine. I don't want to do it but it is what you asked me to do so that you could fulfill your destiny. It is only through pain that we learn our biggest lessons. And it is going to hurt me too. Thank you for making me so brave. I will always love you.">[3]

About 3:00 a.m. I got the call! The baby was born October 27, 2013.

"You're a grandma!" Thomas sounded so happy and proud.

Luckily, I had already warned my boss that I would be taking a week off come the end of October. The baby was on schedule. I drove to Ohio by myself with all the baby gifts loaded into my Nissan Altima. The drive was long but not difficult to navigate. I have never paid much attention to people's color but once in Ohio, I became acutely aware of my whiteness.

Arriving at the home, I approached a glass-enclosed porch and spied a thin older woman assisted by a cane slowly shuffling toward me. Her hair was wildly loose without much gray at all for her aged appearance. In fact, her skin was quite beautiful, and her kindness was evident in her eyes. Mavie, Thomas' great grandma graciously greeted me, it made me really wonder why Starre felt so uncomfortable with her. I had to stop by the house to unload enough stuff to be able to fit the new parents and their infant into my car.

"Oh," spoke Mavie, in a bit of a surprise, not actually recognizing the stranger at her patio door. "You must be Starre's mom," she said through the glass. I know our family resemblance is remarkable but I giggled to myself, realizing that it must have felt a little strange for her to have an unknown white person knocking at her door. I let her know of my intention to pick up her first great, great grandchild, but had to unload my back seat before heading to the hospital.

I slowly met the relatives and unlike Starre was able to feel quite at ease with all of them. I was really impressed with Thomas' family, and how they graciously welcomed us into their home.

---

[3] <text> My conception of each child's inner dialogue with their mom as they were born.

The baby was named Jamez Thomas Smith. His adorable presence made his parents so very happy, their faces glowed with pride. The infant made a great-great grandma out of quiet Mavie, and *her* daughter became a great grandma–Bonnie was blessed with beautiful, big expressive eyes. Thomas' mom, the paternal grandmother, Dorice, seemed a gentle soul and kept her hair neatly back in a bun. There were also a couple of aunts and uncles. We all enjoyed the precious new baby. Everyone was so generous and brought even more gifts. We took lots of pictures of baby Jamez and his family which included five generations! When I first met Bonnie, I knew I was going to like her right away. She was a full-figured woman, very dark complexion, with short black curly hair; a heart of gold and very sassy.

"Give me some of that sugar!" She said as she held her arms up to receive Jamez.

I was able to spend lots of time with the baby and Starre, helping her organize all of the clothes and baby things. Jamez took immediate interest in being read stories. He sat mesmerized while daddy read to him. I had taken Starre to the first pediatrician visit where I actually witnessed her standoffish behavior when the pediatrician mentioned vaccinations. I spoke with her further on that subject, but could feel her resistance. I took her food shopping and she rode around on a motorized scooter picking out the items on her grocery list. The week went by all too fast.

That first week, while my mom was in Ohio with us, I was still having a really hard time sitting. The nurses at the hospital thought I was being overly dramatic, but something still did not feel right. I found a small handheld mirror and went into the bathroom to look at my vagina more carefully. What I discovered was a small shred of skin about pinky size hanging from the edge of my birth canal! I was shocked and pissed that the midwife did not see this and sew it up right away. I knew it was because they had asked me to push against my body's will. I called in my mom and she agreed that I should have it checked out at the doctors. I wanted this thing fixed ASAP! No wonder I was so sore!

I ended up seeing a surgeon that felt it was too late to stitch it up. She told me to give it six weeks, that it would become less swollen and eventually look fine. I was still mad.

CHAPTER 10

This is when things slowly started to change. The new mama was very protective of baby Jamez. She really didn't want anyone to hold him. Sometimes new moms are a bit neurotic, nothing *anyone* does is right. They don't hold him right, they don't feed him right, and they don't burp him right, etc.

My Starre was super shy about her breast feeding. No one could be in the room and if anyone walked in she ran into the bathroom with the baby at her breast. She told the relatives that everything they said was negative and a bad influence on the baby. Thomas was too rough as dads tend to be and when he couldn't console the crying, Starre immediately tried to get Jamez back. TV was not allowed either. I guess all this made Thomas unhappy and insecure. The couple *had* gone to parenting classes but the actually sharing of the baby and respect for each other's parenting style was never addressed as I think most families can work through that part amiably.

All in all, they made the best of things. The relatives visited often even though they were being shunned by Starre. Mavie got to hold the baby a lot and even babysat a couple of times. Jamez' first Christmas was celebrated at great aunt Terry's home in Michigan. Terry was Bonnie's daughter whom I've never met. They all drove out together and spent the week visiting and crooning with baby Jamez. Terry even got professional photos taken, everything appeared happy on the surface.

As it happened one day when Jamez was about four months old and having a crying spell while his dad was watching him, Starre tried to take control. Thomas was frustrated and ended up giving in by dropping the baby onto their bed. Starre took a fit and from this point on their lives changed forever!

In retrospect, I can now see that my Starre's relationship with Thomas was very green and that that kind of young love through inexperience beckons to superiority. Their love hadn't endured enough time to prove itself and it was ruled with insecurity.

My little mama, not wanting to call Dorice again called the police. I don't know why she does that—it always seems to cause more harm than good. I think it was just too overwhelming for her being in a strange town with relatives she was not too sure of, and a romantic partner she was definitely not too sure of anymore. Anyway, when the police and the EMS came to the house, Starre told them what had happened and even though Jamez seemed okay, they wanted to have him checked out at the hospital.

Starre and Jamez were brought to the hospital, courtesy of Cleveland's finest. Fortunately, the baby's physical check was fine, and the X-rays taken were unremarkable. Unfortunately, when something like this occurs, Child Protective Services (CPS) are called in. Starre was told that she could not return home with the baby. She was frantic and called her best friend, Amelia.

Dorice had offered up her home for a refuge, but Starre didn't know that until after Amelia had bought a non-refundable bus ticket to MA.

Starre really didn't want to leave Thomas but she felt stuck. Not only did it put Starre and the baby in jeopardy with child services, but it left Thomas feeling abandoned. Little did we know that this was a recurring theme in his life, and it was marked with severe trust issues as well. As it turned out, this event hindered their trust even further, and the couple's relationship failed miserably.

My Starre had called to keep me abreast of what was happening; I was distraught. I really didn't understand the impact of CPS but felt it was all blown out of proportion. In one sense, it was great that I would be able to see my grandson more often, but not having a permanent place to live was not so good.

Along with the bus ticket, Amelia opened up her home and shared a bedroom with Starre and baby Jamez. She gave them one month to figure things out.

This was hard on everyone. I had just gotten married to Joe two weeks before Jamez was born, so not only was I a newlywed, but as I mentioned before, we had a very tiny home that we rented. It was difficult for me to say "no" to Starre but knowing all I had sacrificed for her already, I knew I just couldn't do it and there was no way I could put my new husband in the position to take in a new mama and her child either, even if it was my one and only grandchild. It often makes me sad knowing that if I was still married to her dad, it would have been absolutely no problem at all. In fact, we would have jumped at the chance as we had a large five-room apartment. But alas, life goes on the way we choose it, and this would have defeated Starre's spiritual purpose here on the earth. Her life has unfolded exactly the way it was supposed to and as planned even before her earthly arrival. These unfortunate events have evolved to initiate a lesson and resolve a past life karma, as this *is* Starre's destiny.

The worker from the Ohio Department of CPS drove Jamez and I to the house to collect the necessary items for the trip to MA. We waited in the car for the mandated police escorts to arrive. Mavie did not understand what was happening despite what she had witnessed earlier in the day. She called her daughter Bonnie. I walked up to our room and Thomas was in the bed sleeping. The policeman shined his flashlight at him commanding him to wake up. When he got up, they cuffed him, put on his shoes for him, and escorted him out of the house. I sadly but swiftly began throwing items in the bags the case worker was able to give me. Bonnie showed up and between her and the case worker, I was rushed right out the door in order to catch the bus. I know that rushing people just makes things worse and it was hard to think of everything we would need. Plus, I inevitably lied about having criminal ties in Ohio, I was on probation and shouldn't have left the state at all! Despite the ruckus we arrived at the Greyhound Station just in time.

Jamez was whining for his bottle, and I realized that I had no water to make it!! Luckily, a man on the bus had an unopened bottle of water and was generous enough to give it to us. Still riding the bus the next day, I noticed Jamez looking around at all the people expecting to get their undivided attention that he was used to. It made me realize how secluded we'd become in order to protect ourselves. It was a sad truth for me to observe Jamez with his happy smile saying "Hi" to everyone and no one was even paying attention. This was the beginning of his new life.

After a long trip back to the coast and finally arriving at Amelia's, Starre wanted and needed to retrieve her things that had been left behind. Obviously, she couldn't take it all on the bus. So, elected once again, I took the initiative to rent a van from Sears and asked my son if he could help. I wanted to get to Ohio and back in two days' time, so as not to have to use any vacation time.

On Saturday morning, I drove to Beverly to pick up Sam. I pulled up in front of the house where he was staying and called several times but no answer. I was really anxious to get on the road and my patience was wearing thin. After about twenty minutes, he finally answered and said he'd be right down. It took him another five to seven minutes before he showed. Disheveled and smelling of alcohol, he hopped into my car. I shook my head, as a distant memory popped into my thoughts—the serenity of the day he was born at The North Shore Birth Center in Beverly. In a dimly lit room on a king size bed, just after a sitting in the tub and having water scooped over my belly to calm the pain of labor, he was born naturally.

His dad was so proud to have cut the umbilical cord. I pictured my beautiful newborn son resting in my arms like a precious gift. I smiled with the memory of how sweet and innocent he was even as a toddler. My handsome Sam was a good boy, he had a big heart and was always a very hard worker. I was proud to be his mom. He definitely kept his core values through his shortened life but it saddened my heart to see his essence had become so shrouded with alcohol.

"So, when you getting sober Sam?" I know he disliked me saying that, but I felt obliged and secretly hoped maybe someday it would sink in.

"It is what it is Mah, it is what it is. You know I love my vodka"

"It doesn't mean I have to like it."

We drove straight to Sears in Peabody to pick up the rental van. After another minor snafu there, we finally headed out to gather Starre and Jamez in Andover and soon were on our way to Ohio. The eleven-hour drive went well, but we didn't arrive in Cleveland until about 10:00 p.m. that evening.

Mavie was again gracious in allowing us to stay the night before packing everything up in the morning. This whole situation was emotionally draining on everyone. Thomas and his relatives were heartbroken.

That night, Thomas and I slept on the dining room floor with Jamez close by in his crib. We let my brother, Sam, sleep in our bed and my mom stayed on the couch downstairs where she had previously slept when she stayed the week Jamez was born. The next morning, Thomas made us breakfast that included salmon.

Somehow we found space in the van for everything including the fish! Sam remarked, as we drove off, how devastated Thomas looked. He was watching his family leave him for a second time in a matter of less than two weeks.

We got back east by 8:00 p.m. Sunday. With many helping hands, the van was emptied in twenty minutes. It was decided that I would keep the bird and the cat.

During the stay in Andover, the CPS case was transferred to MA. Starre was completely honest with the social worker even stating she was not afraid of the baby's father. The social worker told her she was better off not sharing that information. Eventually the case was closed once she knew Starre had benefits and a pediatrician.

After the four weeks were up, Starre was able to move in with her uncle, my brother in Beverly.

Before long, Thomas' broken heart caused him to follow Starre to MA via rental car. My brother reluctantly took Thomas in as well. The situation was not very amiable. It seemed Thomas was thought of in the same light as when he had come to Georgetown—unappreciative, unhelpful, and basically outright rude at times. Eventually, he was asked to leave.

Thomas found a shelter where he could stay. Starre spent nights at her uncle's, spending her days at the library and visiting with Thomas. One Saturday my angel wanted to cook dinner for me and showed up with Jamez and Thomas. We had an awesome afternoon walking around Salem and a luscious dinner, all prepared by Starre; the girl who didn't cook! She used to call me to ask how to make even simple things like scrambled eggs! Things took a little longer as they tend to when an infant is involved. Joe, a barber in Boston, works on Saturdays and was due to come home around 6:00. We were not quite done eating and knowing how he felt about Thomas, I thought I should give him a warning. He was irate, but I didn't get the full message as his phone died in the middle of it. The trio left on foot shortly thereafter.

There was a scene when Joe finally got home. It seems I had forgotten that Joe did not want Thomas in our house *ever again*.

CHAPTER 11

Joe was livid, like I said, but his unfinished message left me no clue as to how angry he really was. I had tried to call back but his phone just went dead. It seemed Joe was not coming home, thinking Thomas was still here. Of course Thomas, Starre, and baby Jamez had pretty much left right after my call. Due to my inability to let him know, Joe didn't come home until after 10:00 p.m. He stormed straight upstairs to where I was in the bedroom. I saw the anger in his face as he yelled at me.

"Didn't you get my message?"

"No, it cut off." I was shaking. Joe had *never* shouted at me before. I had never seen him this mad. I followed him downstairs and to my dismay, he grabbed the birdcage with the dove in it and threw it out the door! The cat litter and the cat were next! I was flabbergasted!

I ended up pleading with him to let the cat stay the night. I promised to get her out the next day. He finally agreed, and I found Buggy and brought her and the litter box back in. I was able to put the bird cage and all in my car as she was a "pigeon" so to speak, and I knew the cold wouldn't hurt her. I cleaned up the litter from the back porch and consoled Buggy for a little while.

The following day was trying.

I called Starre. "I have to get the cat and bird out of here. Joe blew up last night."

Everyone was still sleeping at my brother's house, so she couldn't ask if it was okay to bring them there. I'm sure she heard the desperation in my voice.

"Just bring them over, Bummy."

When I got there, Jamez was in a child seat accompanied by Starre's laptop entertaining with educational songs. This was how she kept him busy so she could attend to her own business. It made me a little sad, as I felt he should be experiencing the tenderness of human touch and even doing physical activities like crawling.

My brother already had a cat and a dog. I guess Starre moved the cat inside, keeping her in the carrier and put the bird out back so she could leave to go see Thomas. When my brother saw the pets, he blew his top! Needless to say it was a complete disaster! He called me and bitched me out and when his sweet little niece returned, he threw her out on her butt! Homeless, she joined Thomas at the shelter.

Their up and down relationship was causing a lot of trouble. Thomas in his determination to have Starre relive the pain he felt when she left with their child, found ways to push her buttons by walking off with Jamez, and making verbal threats. Due to a melee at a mall one day, while Thomas tried to take control, CPS stepped in again! They were staying here, there, and everywhere for a couple of weeks using credit that wasn't their own. All I can say is, "setting up a lifestyle as a thief can only by karma evolve into being the object of thievery." The pair consulted with services in Beverly and Gloucester and almost got placed but for the fact that Jamez was not vaccinated. This is when they decided to be evasive, leaving out that fact from future prospects.

I tried to convince her let Thomas go so she could get some kind of housing. "You just can't have it both ways Starre, if Thomas won't step up to the plate and get a job, then the only way to get permanent shelter for you and Jamez is to go to DHHS and hope for the best. I mean, you really need to think of Jamez in a healthy way. I know you have a preconceived picture of the perfect world in which a child has a mom and a dad, but if the dad is unstable it may be best for you and the child to move on. It's a very difficult choice."

My saddened and worn out Starre set up a meeting with a social worker at my home in Salem. After Joe and I left for work, Starre took up temporary residence with baby Jamez and the pets while waiting for the case worker to arrive. She played her cards right, telling the complete truth including that she didn't feel Thomas to be a threat and the social worker referred her to HAWC (Help for Abused Women and Children). Starre told me that the social worker felt she was a good mom and the move would keep her and the baby safe despite her feelings toward the dad.

When I got home from work, I almost died—I was faced with finding somewhere for the pets AGAIN!! Bonnie called right when I had walked in the door, and I was a wreck, I just couldn't deal with helping Thomas, I couldn't think straight. I didn't want to upset my husband again and had to figure out my own situation. I felt absolutely terrible that I couldn't bring Thomas to Boston where Bonnie could set him up with a train ticket to go home to Ohio. What a complete mess these two had gotten themselves into. I did agree to bring Thomas his suitcase which had been placed behind our back porch. He was waiting right uptown at a gas station. I was so sorrowful with this bleak situation. I had no words for Thomas, I knew his heart was broken again. He just looked at me with a somber expression and said,

"I *do* love her."

Somehow, I knew that to be true. In retrospect, I had wished that I had at least thought to give Thomas a little money, but I was just too frantic. I felt that I had let both him and Bonnie down after all she and her family had done for us.

Starre was being put up for the night in a hotel at the other end of Beverly and told me I could bring the cat and the bird and the remainder of Jamez' belongings to her there.

The next morning I had to return to the hotel to retrieve the pets as they were not allowed where she was being placed. To my dismay, this was an undisclosed location and there would be no contact with her at all. This was a "safe" house. I was not even allowed to know the city where she would be. When I walked in, Starre was bathing Jamez. I was impressed how she had learned to improvise. She was standing in the tub with Jamez sitting between her feet to stabilize him while she washed him. It was another woebegone goodbye, my only consolation was knowing she and my grand-baby would be cared for and safe.

"Take care sweetie, I love you so much. I think you have made the right choice."

"I know Mah. I love you too."

I called Sunny and desperately asked her if she could take the bird and the cat for a day or two. My first born savior said she would, I was so relieved!

CHAPTER 12

How about happy beginnings,
Ain't that how they start?
Why would you indulge?
If there wasn't a joyful spark
Familiarized with the characters;
Binded by the direction
Danger becomes apparent,
Yet my mind can't intercept it

I was dropped off at North Station in Boston where I was to take the train to a nearby town. I had Jamez in my front carrier, a huge bag of our things in the stroller, and his walker hanging from the stroller handles. I was told that when I got there I was to walk to the nearest payphone and call the police to pick me up. I finally arrived at the shelter by dark and settled into a room with Jamez. The room was small and there were two twin beds in it, a dresser, and a table. I asked for a pack-n-play for Jamez to sleep in, and I set that up in between the two beds, its sides touching each mattress. Our window had bars on it for safety. The next day I met the other girls who stayed there but pretty much kept to Jamez and myself. Jamez and I played in the playroom they had for kids. He used his walker in the hallway and kitchen. Another girl got visits with her son who was about a year old. We were free to go and stay as we pleased, but had to ring a bell to get back inside and were given no key. I think our curfew was nine p.m. The other thing was, our phones and computers had to be shut off and were taken and put into a locked drawer. We had to ask for our devices and could only use them outside within a certain radius from the shelter during the daytime.

One day, I was texting with Thomas. I had written a five-year goal plan that didn't include Thomas, but this was one of the only things I looked forward to. I even started looking for family shelters outside of HAWC. We were also allowed a certain length of phone time on their landline in a closed room, something I did not share with my mom.

I remember I was moved into a room with a crib in it after another girl got kicked out because she was talking with her man. I put up pictures that inspired me and had a flower on my windowsill. Jamez and I would go out into the yard, and I would show him the different types of trees. I was really happy. We were allowed to keep food in the basement refrigerator and took turns making dinner on a weekly list.

It was during this time, I had begun to see a small bulging in lower part of Jamez' belly. When I touched it with a little pressure, it seemed to disappear. I consulted with Louise Hay's, You can Heal Your Life, it stated that a hernia represents "ruptured" relationships. I firmly believed that I should try to make it work with Thomas for our baby's well-being.

After only a couple of weeks, Thomas texted me something that indicated he was coming back to MA. I felt emotions of excitement run though my body and a sense that he really loved us. The next day he was in town. Jamez and I left for the grocery store with the walker hanging from the stroller handles. I spotted Thomas walking toward us, and I was very happy to see him. We hugged for a few minutes, and then he told me how he had gotten here.

Another red flag, I chose to ignore! He stole the car from a dealership! When the salesman went inside to do a credit check, Thomas saw the keys in the ignition and took it as a sign that the car was his. I did not leave the shelter right away, so it was very stressful for Thomas as he was sleeping in the *car, sometimes moving in the middle of the night. We ate at food shelters, and I still visited the library with Jamez during the day. One night I came home late for my 9:00 curfew. They told me it was a bit late for me to be staying out all day with a newborn and questioned if I was talking to my "abuser." I told then I really appreciated all they had done for me but I would be leaving in the morning.*

We stayed at a friend's house for a couple of days but it wasn't working out; the atmosphere was too toxic with smoking and loud arguments so we became homeless again. One day a worker at a food shelter overheard that we were sleeping in the car and called the police. We were on the run again!

I did not hear a word or any news for over a month. I think it was about mid-April when I got a call from my girl. She had left the safe house and hooked up with Thomas once again! They were making the rounds collecting all their belongings from the places they had stayed and saying good bye to all their friends and family. They had planned to go to Presque Isle, Maine where Starre had a former girlfriend who thought they may be able to get an apartment above her and her family.

They met me outside of my office in a well-packed Crown Victoria. Jamez was safe in his car seat, but my little mama took him out so I could hold him and kiss him goodbye. I hugged my daughter and Thomas as well.

"You take care of my babies," I ordered.

I didn't see Starre Grace for her birthday or hear another word until August. I was at the airport with Joe when I received the most devastating phone call of my entire life.

"Life has been very hard for me since I left Cleveland," she began. "We've been in and out of shelters." She choked up on the words and burst into tears. "They took away my baby in June. And while I'm spilling my guts, you might as well know that I am pregnant again."

"WHAT?! NO STARRE!!!!! NO!!! I mean, NO, this can't be. This can't be real. NO." I shook with inner sobs, I was so stunned, I couldn't think of what to say. She gave me the number for the social worker, hoping I could talk some sense into her and the Department. I couldn't believe she was alive telling me this, how could she function? No wonder it took her two months to call me. I felt her pain so deeply it made me cry, I wanted to scream to the heavens but at the same time selfishly all I could do was feel my own broken heart. It felt as if it was broken right in half, and yet I really didn't know what I felt at all. I kept it all in, I absolutely couldn't even confide in Joe. This was too big, more than I could handle. I think in some way I felt ashamed that this could happen to my family. The sadness exploded inside me like a cancer, a giant green monster with its arms raised up high in a menacing threat to destroy me. It's big, hairy green paws were grabbing at my neck, choking me, taking my breath away. Roaring at the top of its lungs sending shock waves of fear through my body. I remained numb to the reality which made it manageable to lock the terror inside me while I remained composed on the outside. A miraculous feat indeed. I was supposed to be happy—we were on our way to Vegas, although I couldn't help but feel the horror of death inside of me, reaching up clenching the life from my heart, knowing the suffering that my child was enduring. I did try the social worker Kris, but had to leave a message.

Once in Vegas, I couldn't make the call right away but along about the second day while we were at the pool, I sorted things out in my head. It took me quite a while to muster up the courage and get to a point where I could think rationally. Kris was not very sympathetic and obviously this wasn't the time to plead with her. I asked her to please return Jamez to his mama as soon as possible so that he wouldn't be emotionally damaged. I couldn't keep my tears back especially after she coldly told me it would take at least a year to conduct their investigation. Horrified, I felt completely helpless, I didn't understand how all this could happen to my own child. A child raised in love who protected her baby with every fiber of her being. We left it that I would call her back when I returned home. And so I tried my best to enjoy our temporary diversion from reality.

It's always such a disappointment to return to work after a wonderful vacation. As I drove my Altima over the Beverly-Salem Bridge, I noticed the tide was extremely low. A large rock encrusted sandbar jutted above the surface to the right and was topped with a stationary, pyramid-shaped granite marker topped with a red flag, warning boaters to stay in the channel to the right. I continued on toward Beverly taking the scenic route past the ocean as was my usual drive to work. When I drove past Dane Street Beach, I remarked to myself that it was "walk-over-to-Lynch Park low!" As I had dubbed the lowest of tides in my hometown.

Reluctantly, I took my last breath of fresh air and went into work. The freedom of time and mind ease was soon to be a thing of the past. Suddenly and quite violently, my mind became cluttered with details, worries, schedules, and deadlines of my job. Patient complaints of their struggles with physical and financial worries laid heavy burdening my compassionate heart and the stress began to settle into my stiffening body. Dealing with insurance companies and attorneys and phone calls! "Ugh," and the worst was yet to come—the dreaded phone call to Kris.

Mid-morning, I got up from my desk and left the office to make my call. It was more private in the hallway where I could walk or head outside. I reached her on the first try. We went through some back ground information first. Then she started asking more private questions which I answered truthfully.

"Did you know she's pregnant again?" she asked, like it was some kind of crime.

"Yes, I know."

Kris also told me another story about a scene in Presque Isle that had raised some concern in regard to Starre and Thomas being "fit" parents. It seemed Thomas, for the second time tried to take off with the baby.

I wanted to know if I could see my grandson at one of Starre's upcoming visitations. Kris told me I would have to be cleared for that. She urged me to attend what's call an FTM--Family Team Meeting. I was mostly concerned with the emotional well-being of Jamez.

"How do you justify stealing a child from his mother's arms? A mother–child bond is so important to a child's self-esteem. His heart must be so overwhelmed with grief."

Kris responded by telling me, "It's good for a child to have several love bonds. It's like loving a mother and a grandmother." Then she went into some meaningless details of Starre and Thomas' tumultuous relationship. She also agreed with me that dropping a baby onto a bed was not necessarily dangerous or abusive. I wish I had that on tape!

The remark about several love bonds put me over the edge with her, I decided that Kris was a troubled soul—cold and heartless; I mean maybe it was just part of her job, but it left me bewildered.

Kris took advantage of my openness and next asked me what I thought about the car Thomas and Starre were driving.

"I don't know, why?" I queried.

"Well where do you think they got it from?"

"I mean, I don't know, he probably stole it," I said. I know that was not the best thing to say, but I was completely drained and done with her grilling me. (I actually had no idea that that was the truth.) It's a funny thing about stealing; I think people who steal are actually trying to replace the love they were never given at a certain early age. It has to do with emotional development and the first and/or second chakra; age womb to two years.[4]

---

[4] Chakras--energies centers within the body aligned with the spine and associated with color. Starting at the base of the spine—the root chakra, red, first year of life, physical identity. The second chakra is located just below the belly button called the sacral chakra, orange, 6 months-2 years of age, representing emotional identity. Third—just above the belly button, yellow, power, 18 months-3 ½ years representing the ego. Fourth—the heart center, green, 3 ½-7 years, social identity. Fifth—throat, blue, 7-12 years, creative identity. Sixth—third eye, purple or indigo, 12 and above, representing self-reflection. Lastly, the crown chakra which connects us with the divine.

After I had hung up, I was dazed. I felt as though I had been violated, I knew I had said too much for my own good.

At this point in August, Starre was keeping me up to date with all that had been going on.

When they arrived in Presque Isle, yes, the apartment above her friend's was open but they could not rent it as they had no money.

They found a shelter and Starre was quite content for a bit. That is until Jamez was abruptly taken, she said he was kept in police custody for a week. During that week Starre's only reason for living was the thought of getting her baby back. She busied herself with faxing WIC agencies, shelters, photocopying healthcare cards, printing up library book lists that she checked out, and collecting as much evidence as she could to win the case. She also told me she had set up a doctor's appointment for Jamez and had been going to couples counseling prior to Jamez' removal. When they arrived at court for the hearing, they met with their lawyers separately.

I was urging for the hearing but Thomas' attorney was advising differently. He told Thomas that everything would be taken as factual and Thomas could not accept the fact that he had dropped the baby onto the bed as abusive! So he waived the hearing! I busted out in tears, I ran to the restroom and didn't want to come out. My lawyer came in and told me the judge was waiting and I would have to go in. I cleaned myself up as best I could but was filled with more anger than I want to admit. I walked into the courtroom and saw… her—the lady who took Jamez. "You like taking people's kids away huh?!" Of course the judge was not impressed. I took my seat and flicked off a tear from each eye like rolling glass marbles. I had prepared and counted on winning our case that day! It was a huge mistake to waive the hearing because now they had all kinds of time to collect and distort their evidence into whatever they needed.

She was being "allowed" visitations and it was torture. They were held at a place called HCI, a small 10" by 10" room. Watching Jamez leave time after time, trying to tell him she would be right here as she pointed to her

61

heart. It hurt so much to see him because she knew she had let him down. She found she was crying before, after or during the visits. It was like she was losing Jamez over and over again.

Jamez had been placed in a foster home where the mom and dad worked all day! He attended daycare for ten hours a day! I just couldn't believe the Department could separate a child from his mama and place him in a daycare all day. He needed a warm, loving, and understanding person to comfort him while he adjusted to this horrific trauma he was facing. My heart was breaking for my grandbaby. Jamez' new family had an older boy that joined him at the daycare which must have given him some comfort. Unfortunately, I guess some kind of problem arose and Kris decided to place Jamez in a new daycare away from his newly acquired foster brother. Starre and I were devastated at the amount of times this child's heart was torn apart.

I had decided to reach out to the ombudsman. An ombudsman is someone who works with parents who are concerned with the happenings between their child and DHHS. They can help if a parent thinks their rights are being interfered with or if the parent disagrees with the plan developed by the caseworker. I was given a name but it was very hard to even schedule a time to speak with her. When our conversation ended, she blatantly told me she would contact DHHS—not Starre! It seemed like another dead end.

Meanwhile, the department must have decided that the original foster family was not a good match and once again moved Jamez to a new foster family where the mother was a stay-at-home mom. This made us feel somewhat better but didn't change how we felt about his tender little heart being broken so many times. How dare the Department claim they were protecting a child when his emotional well-being was being damaged over and over. The emotional factor should be just as important as the physical. Both are highly important to a child's well-being. After all, what is a body without a soul? Also, with my knowledge of the chakra system, I knew that this kind of damage in a child's first year would most certainly manifest as "dis-ease" in his later years.

The new foster mom's name was Helen. Starre and I thought this would be a good thing, but we really didn't know what went on behind the scene. The Department seemed to be working more closely with Helen, pursuing weekly home visits and taking inventory on all the child's needs, as well as Helen's responses to his care. Clearly, Helen knew much more about the ins and outs of DHHS, which already gave her an advantage over Starre. Eventually, we kind of felt that Helen was out to steal Jamez' heart and keep him for her own. He was calling her "mom" while Starre was just some sort of babysitter that he saw once or twice a week. It must have been very confusing for him. Starre's insecurities were causing her more anguish and she felt that Helen was always making herself out to be the perfect mom, not realizing that it upshot Starre's inexperience and made her feel incompetent. I saw first-hand that the Department played on this as well. There was never any talk that Starre was his real mom and sometimes it seemed that Helen was not always forthright or accommodating to Starre, simply because she was following protocol. I secretly felt that Helen feigned sickness for herself or Jamez in order to skip a few of the visitations. I know it was a huge inconvenience for her to drive for an hour only to have to kill two hours during the visit and then drive another hour back home. The situation was actually very difficult for both parties and I knew for sure that our judgmental attitudes were unfair. Jamez was too young to understand the concept of "mom" and of course, Helen *was* not only far more experienced but quite naturally wanted to give Jamez all the love she could. It probably didn't seem right for Jamez to call her something different than what the other children in her home call her.

Starre was doing her best to make the visitations in the small room at HCI seem more natural. It was here she got to express her creative spirit while engaging in play with her child. She told me how since she could not have outside visits, she and Thomas actually brought "the beach" to Jamez. They had filled a sheet with sand and brought along some beach toys.

Before Thomas stopped attending visitations altogether, Mom and Dad were making positive strides toward reunification. In October, she sent me pictures of a visitation where she had brought a pile of leaves for Jamez to jump into. Starre was determined to share her "outdoor" upbringing with her baby and it also helped to soften the "awkwardness" of the visitation.

CHAPTER 13

It's as clear as a gunshot
As sad as the ceasing of an infant's life
Why is there still hope?
Despite such a strife

I got some time off in September to go to Maine for the second day of the jeopardy hearing. Starre needed some support as Thomas had declined to be involved with any part of the court proceedings. Starre and I just couldn't understand any of his reasoning, it was becoming clear that he had some deep-seeded mental issues. He had found a job, which initially kept him from the visitations with his son, but to not take time off for a court hearing where the serious decision of his son's future was at stake seemed a complete lapse in judgment. I guess this is where I began to realize that Thomas himself must have suffered a similar trauma as a child causing him severe emotional distress and where his trust issues first began. Fortunately, for him he always had family to step in. I could only imagine that emotionally he was removing himself for his own protection.

Anyway, I got to Maine safely and found the courthouse. I went upstairs and sat around for about an hour not really knowing which courtroom Starre was in.

Finally, a tall woman came out of one of the courtroom doors. She was of medium build with her dark hair cut in a short bob. She was wearing a black pantsuit and heels. She towered over me as she walked closer to the bench I was sitting on.

"Are you Starre's mother?"

"Yes."

"I'm Kris," she said with authority.

Her height and stature made me feel insignificant. She coldly assured me they were almost done and then went back in. I was glad for that, I really didn't want to engage in any further conversation with her as I felt the impact similar to a colonoscopy.

Eventually, everyone filed out of the courtroom. Starre was wearing a pretty flowery dress and low heels. She was accompanied by her attorney. Pam was an average to short woman with wavy ash blonde hair, she had a soft smile. Starre was visibly distraught and had been crying. She told me that there had been talk of Jamez' hernia. Kris had taken the stand stating that it would be beneficial to massage his penis! Starre was horrified out of her wits, they had already torn him away from his mama which she felt was the cause of the hernia as it represents ruptured relationships but now they were making talk of what she considered to be sexual abuse!! The appalling fact that Starre had not brought Jamez to the pediatrician regarding his hernia was coupled with the admission that she herself suggested that when it bulges, she simply pushes it back. (That fact had been taken out of context. Starre reported to me that she had done that at the very beginning when the bulge was tiny.) I felt so saddened that her medical decisions had effected Jamez so severely. She told authorities that she believed in visualization, homeopathic treatments and that the mind has the ability to heal any dysfunctions in the body. I was a bit dismayed that I was the person who had introduced her to that mindset. I had no idea that she had taken information from one or two books and adopted those concepts as a doctrine for her life and that of a child's. While I didn't strictly follow that guidance myself, knowing I was not trained or certified in any of the techniques, I do believe it to be "possible." I had even given it a try a couple times with my own children before going to the doctor at a time when we were without a car and I found it uncomfortable to ask for rides.

Pam was very supportive and compassionate. She had tried her absolute best in Starre's behalf but without the dad there, it just didn't seem like a united effort of two parents desperately seeking to have their child returned. Thomas was found in jeopardy for abandonment—(failing to appear at the hearing) and physical abuse—(that of dropping Jamez onto a bed and there was some mention that he had been physical with Starre herself). The court also found fault in his evasiveness stating, "He uses and insists on being called a variety of other names. He refuses to disclose his legal name, date of birth and social security number and other personally identifying information." Although, he was found to have felony conviction in the state of Michigan from which he has an outstanding arrest warrant for probation.

Thomas somehow felt that the state owned and controlled him especially in monetary situations just by his registered birth name on his birth certificate. He felt due to his child being taken, that that in itself was controlling his present and future life. In his head by not using a legal name, he felt exempt from following their rules and therefore they couldn't tell him what to do.

Starre was also found in jeopardy. They documented the incident in Cleveland as a possible flight risk while and clearly stating, "she elected to accept a free bus ticket from Ohio protectives services" for her return to family in MA. She was faulted for remaining with the father, fleeing from MA to Maine and not disclosing to the shelters that the baby was unvaccinated. The pair left the shelter from Presque Isle, Maine and travelled to Portland, so now she's a proven flight risk. The fact that she was again pregnant, and had a bizzare belief system was a giant setback that followed Starre like a shadow for the next two years. Unfortunately, Starre in her traumatized state of mind sent the Guardian ad Litem (GAL), Storm an email that gave the whole system a blitz of bewilderment regarding her "belief system." He also felt that Starre while being loving and caring for Jamez, didn't seem to have been bringing him to scheduled pediatric appointments. All in all, not a pretty picture, even I felt destroyed after reading the jeopardy order—they sure know how to build a case.

"Exhibit one" had detailed some of the philosophical garbage that Starre had emailed the GAL. Stating things like, "if a child dies it is the choice of the universe." I mean what was she thinking? It is true that many people believe all things happen for a reason and therein lies the lesson, but to send something like this to the one person who is in charge of deciding the well-being of your child seems to portray utter carelessness. I hope, quite possibly that Starre did this to take a step back, to convince herself that it didn't matter because she actually didn't have any hope in reunification. I for one wish that those words never reached the GAL's desktop, knowing full well that those specific words gave everyone involved doubts that Starre was actually sane.

There was also talk that Jamez was small for his age and concern that his legs were not developed properly. In reality, he was the spitting image of his dad, skinny legs and all.

Starre and her attorney had made no headway with the seemingly unjust, one sided department's argument against reunification. Around that time, it was made known to me that the judge bases his ruling solely on the department's recommendations, giving no credence to the parents' thoughts, words or actions. So the endless fight began.

Pam was removing herself from the case. She was in over her head and she accepted the defeat. The Department of Health and Human Services' mandate was final. She had the foresight to know that she was out of her league and did not have enough power to fight this clearly unbalanced court of law. The winds of change have spoken and a set of unfortunate events continues on.

Starre was given a nine point bulleted list of things she needed to achieve before any thoughts of reunification would even be considered. The list included things like counseling, parenting classes, a CODE evaluation and stated clearly in the court order was this, "shall approve such vaccinations as are deemed essential by the pediatrician."

Focusing on the positive and feeling blessed with another beautifully sunny fall day, I met up with my brave and undaunted little cherub at her newly chosen attorney's office. Nikki was a pretty gal with medium length dark curly hair. She was a petite woman, but her size was no match for her people skills, compassion and knowledge. She had a real grasp on Starre's pursuit of reunification. She realized in just this one meeting with her client that Starre was so damaged by the separation of her child that she was not clearly thinking about what was being presented to her. In other words, she was not fully comprehending the questions put forth by the Department, and so her answers in return were not expressed properly or understood either. This was one of the reasons how the whole situation got misinterpreted and a "delusional" tag was soon put on Starre's head by the mandated CODE evaluation.

We ate lunch outside at a Mexican restaurant. The sun was hot but we were shaded by an umbrella which made it quite comfortable. My girl ate like a ravenous mom eating for two. It made me worry if she was getting enough food.

From there we went straight to the FTM where I got to see Kris, the social worker in action. Without her heels, she stood just a bit taller than myself. We gathered in a small, all white meeting room around a rectangular table. Kris, the leader by default, sat on one side with her partner in crime, the GAL, Storm. He was dressed professionally in a tailored black suit which I think may have disguised his excess weight a bit. Nikki and Starre shared the smaller end to my right and a man, Paul who was Thomas' appointed attorney sat to my left, unaccompanied by his client.

I sat directly across from Kris and Storm. Thomas' Aunt Terry whom I believed had raised him as a teen also attended by speaker phone.

Kris' bangs kept falling in her face and her nails were badly bitten. Right off the bat, she made a comment about Thomas' unusual behavior regarding his name. The negative banter went forward between Kris and Storm. I listened for a while, but finally had to ask, "Do you really think dropping a child on a bed is reason enough to take him away from his parents?"

Storm replied stating that the department had done nothing wrong.

"I mean, these alleged allegations against my child seem laughable, how do you justify Thomas' actions to be life-threatening, dangerous or violent? Or not having a child vaccinated a crime?" Clearly, I was ignoring *all* the facts in the jeopardy order.

"The actions that have occurred are serious violations, and it is not something *we* have done but rather Starre has put upon herself."

There was no point in arguing, he casually remained unemotional and had put me in my place, so I decided to keep to myself for the remainder of the meeting.

Kris was getting irritated as the two attorneys were also questioning the Department's motives in defense of the parents. Both Nikki and Paul were great in their clients' behalf engaging in thought provoking conversations with the Department.

At the end, I was compelled to thank Paul for his attendance and defense of an absent client. It really meant a lot to us.

When Starre and I got outside, I asked her about Kris. I just couldn't understand how she could be doing this job. Starre told me that she had questioned Kris in the same way and that her answer was, "I love my job." Wow, I just didn't get it.

I would like to make a note to please excuse my negative judgments as to the attitudes of those who work at the Department of Health and

Human Services. I do understand that people doing their jobs have a certain standard to abide by and my perception is only due to my position of where I am in the scheme of these things.

CHAPTER 14

It's imperative we keep reading
Though some may close the book
Why am I compelled for donating chances?
The choice for logic; praised are crooks

October came with a mix of ups and downs. Starre and Thomas finally got an apartment through GA or general assistance in Portland. This was really good timing because her friend Amelia was also moving. She needed all of Starre's and the baby's things that had been left behind removed from her apartment ASAP as they were heading south to Florida. So of course it was I who stepped in to help. I drove to Andover after work on a Friday evening, and Amelia was great again. She and her boyfriend moved most of the stuff down the three flights and loaded my car to the max. It surprised me that Starre had left so much stuff at her friend's house. Amelia even set up the fish for traveling. I made the trip to Maine the next morning and spent another day with my Starre. We did a little shopping and got a couple new fish to replace the ones that hadn't made it while staying with Amelia.

Later that month, Starre insisted I bring Buggy "home" to her also. It gave me some more quality time with my broken-hearted child. Thomas was also around so the three of us got some food and went down to the waterfront in Portland. They really lived in a great spot, in one direction, they were close to town and public transportation and the other was the beautiful Atlantic Ocean. On the way back, we picked up some furniture for their apartment that had been discarded as trash. As the saying goes, "One man's trash is another man's treasure."

Thomas was not attending visitations, and Starre's emotional state in his absence and the small room in which they were held made for somewhat uncomfortable visits.

Then came another blow. Starre was picked up on a warrant from Ohio because she never finished her community service from their run-in with the law.

So for the second time in her life she spent a week in jail while six months pregnant. I was devastated again, just not the life I pictured for my baby girl, especially after attending college which neither of her siblings even thought was an option. I got the call from Cumberland county jail and received the upsetting news.

Starre was brought to court the very next morning which was a visitation day. She had me email Kris to let her know she wouldn't be able to make the visit, but somehow Kris already knew and showed up at the court! It dawned on me that she had quite possibly initiated the whole scene. It seemed Cuyahoga County down in Ohio wanted Starre back, and I was told they would be coming to get her! None of this made any sense to me at all. That would be a big-time financial expense.

Thomas was also picked up and I was told that the cat was stuck in the house with no food or water! I spoke with someone in charge at the jail who told me I could get the key to their apartment at the front desk. I figured I could leave right after work. When I got there it was dark and I had a heck of a time finding the jail and the actual building where I was supposed to go. Eventually, I did find it and went straight to the main desk only to find out they didn't have the key! I waited a full hour before someone came out to talk to me. This police officer was very kind and knew I had just driven two hours to get a key that was not available. He told me he would try a couple other places and make a few phone calls. He came back a half hour later with still no good news. Being an animal lover, I was deeply concerned and very disheartened that no one even had the courtesy to call and let me know. I went home worried sick about Buggy and Starre.

Luckily, they released Starre after a week. Still, mysteriously no one had a key. My Starre had to walk all the way home and just by chance, the landlord was there to let her in! Buggy had survived! Thomas had actually left a full bowl of dry food and water. Thank God!

Kris took advantage of the situation and stopped all visitations for a full month as the department now had another strike against Starre. Meanwhile, Jamez' first birthday had passed. Starre could only be a part of it through a couple of pictures the foster mom sent.

I went to the next FTM in November and although the spirits were low, visitations were reinstated, and I was finally approved for visiting!

Thomas also decided to join and so in December the three of us went to HCI where the visitations were held.

I got to meet Helen; she seemed quite pleasant. Jamez played with a vacuum while he adjusted to the transition of leaving Helen, whom he called "mom" to spending the next two hours in a small room where he would "visit" with someone familiar named Starre.

"Go see Starre Jamez, she's waiting for you."

He obediently yet somewhat hesitantly filed into the room where Starre, Thomas and I were waiting. It was so good to see him! He was walking! Starre and Thomas had missed this milestone, as well as his first birthday, so I held back to let them take the lead in welcoming him, knowing he probably didn't remember much of me anyway.

The scene seemed really awkward or maybe just emotionally empty. Unfortunately, Starre's subconscious effort to keep that inner volcano dormant erupted onto her tender side as well. Her emotions were absent, she went through the motions of play, but wasn't able to feel any joy or express to Jamez how much she really cherished him. Dad was a little less inhibited, but neither really knew how to truly engage with a loving firm touch, and with a monitor taking notes the whole time, it must have made them even more insecure on how to act. It had been five months since he was taken and it was their first child, they were both so green at parenting and had missed so much, it just didn't seem natural.

Jamez really enjoyed his dad's antics, it was clear how much he loved his dad. Even with such a short visit, there were guidelines to follow. Snack time, diaper changing and time to write in the notebook that Helen and Starre conversed in.

I tried to get Jamez to play with a puzzle, dance and sing, and even tried teaching by pointing to body parts looking for a label, but he really didn't respond to me. It made me sad. Mommy Starre intervened and immediately was able to get some body parts in response. I was told that he had been taught to be wary of strangers, which was probably what I felt like to him.

After snack time, I was able to have him open some presents. I had both birthday and Christmas presents. Again he didn't seem like he was emotionally engaged. He needed coaxing from his mom to get him to open the gifts. He did seem to enjoy them and when he opened the monster pajamas, he laid his head right down on the softness of the fleece. It was so cute and he even said, "Thank you." That was a special gift in itself for me, and I knew he had been taught well.

When the visit was over, Jamez eagerly reunited with Helen and we all said "Bye-bye!"

I drove the parents to the FTM that followed.

I connected with Bonnie through Facetime on my iPad, so she could join the meeting. We had our brief introductions as I faced the iPad around the room so Bonnie could put faces to the names as the team introduced themselves. Kris' supervisor Darla was there. She mostly let Kris take the reins, although her face was very pinched at times.

It wasn't a very productive FTM. I stayed silent as the emotional and verbal abuse directed at Starre and Thomas by each of the presenters was an abomination of humanity. Starre was outwardly undisturbed by the berating, but did speak up for herself, yet not in a defensive manner or as a rebuttal to the allegations.

When the pediatrician visit was brought up, Kris flogged Thomas for his behavior even though it was all hearsay to her. Thomas was very defensive and went off in a long drawn out explanation of what had actually happened in his eyes. He had a way of wearing out a subject until it became threadbare. Kris was losing her cool completely. Not only was she bright red, but she started raising her voice and insulting Thomas verbally. After two hours of this corrupt, chaotic zoo, the meeting was quickly terminated because Kris had another meeting to attend.

Thomas' attorney, myself and Starre hung around for a bit trying to make sense of Thomas' *nonsensical* banter about how his name shouldn't matter, blah, blah, blah. The fact remained that the Department wanted Thomas to get an ID so that he could get a legitimate paternity test, which just seemed like another tactic by DHHS to discredit the parents as they continued to grapple at ways to end the reunification process.

Thomas' attorney had the patience of a saint and finally got Thomas to commit to obtaining the ID. It was settled that Paul would pick Thomas up the following Wednesday and bring him to get it done.

(Needless to say when Wednesday came, Thomas was ill-prepared and the ID never happened.)

After the FTM, we went food shopping. Starre had planned a delightful dinner—lobster bisque and homemade pizza. It seemed Thomas had moved out and was squatting in an empty adjacent apartment. We unpacked the groceries and Starre got the lobster bisque started. It was supposed to simmer for an hour, so I had Starre open her Christmas presents early.

The big present was the laptop my baby girl had asked for. She was psyched! There were a couple of other small presents, as well as gifts from her Grammy and my thoughtful best friend. Starre wanted to keep those for Christmas morning. She had a little tree decorated with lights and ornaments. I felt the magic of Christmas spirit as I opened my gifts from Starre in the darkened room.

The bisque was so elegant, I couldn't believe that Starre had made it! She was always calling me for cooking directions and here she made this bisque better than any restaurant! It was getting too late for me to stick around for the pizza. I was anxious to return home. Starre had me take a giant box filled with gifts for her best friend, Amelia, and her godchild, Amelia's daughter. I was asked to mail it out for her.

I emailed Bonnie that evening to get her take on the FTM. She always had positive and witty thoughts to share but not tonight.

"Kris was quite the spectacle," she wrote. "She was the judge, jury, and executioner all in one!"

CHAPTER 15

2015

In the battlefield of life
She stands erect
Unyielding, meticulous outside
Curdled and soured within

At the beginning of January, I emailed Kris to let her know that I just didn't want to be a part of the FTM's anymore. Not only did I not have unlimited vacation days, but from my perspective there was just too much emotional abuse directed at my already damaged daughter and no forward movement toward reunification whatsoever. A lot of damaging events occurred in the following months. Sometime before Ella was born, Nikki had decided to go into a different branch of law—another hurdle to jump. Also Starre had finally met with the psychologist hired by the Department for a psychological Code evaluation. This is where she was officially diagnosed with Delusional Disorder, Grandiose Type. The clinical definition of delusional is—ideas not based in reality; as thoughts not formed or thought out yet. The doctor put a lot of value on the fact that Starre was determined to use the Internet for information that supported her own beliefs rather than take advice from professionals. From what I understood, this type of diagnosis was more often given to individuals that had no sense of reality and suffered from an acute paranoia psychosis. Either way, quite a discrediting conclusion for my daughter. I was shocked at the implications. Starre's metaphysical beliefs were causing an uproar. I guess it's a little naïveté and the fact that she has no filter on what she shares. This is another giant blow!

I had planned to visit my daughter again toward the end of January but winter began to settle in. January ended with a significant storm dumping three feet of snow on the east coast. February answered with a blizzard, the night Starre went into labor. There was no way I could risk driving to Maine to assist with the home birth that my courageous Starre was planning even though the Department had forewarned her not to go through with it. I knew in a way, it was my angels guiding me.

Thomas stepped in as the birthing coach. Unfortunately, this wasn't the best idea as he was supposed to be out of the picture and now Starre had to keep it a secret.

After not seeing doctors for most of my pregnancy, I was apprehensive that the birth of my second baby was going to be safe.

I met with a pediatrician who was amazing and only recommended a few vaccines. She allowed babies to have their well checks in their parents' arms. She told me that she would come to my home after the birth (since I mentioned having a home birth). While she still thought it was okay, she then mentioned DHHS having a problem with a girl who gave birth at home with only a friend there.

All the professionals I met with, had me fill out releases so that DHHS could speak with them and confirm what I told them.

I met with a homebirth midwife who gave me tips and advice on handling the birth by myself. She had asked what I would do if I couldn't get a midwife to do a homebirth for me. She could tell I was serious and that's when she relayed the most common incidences and what to look out for. Another midwife suggested I use a mirror to observe.

At the team meeting before Ella Rose came, they pretty much told me they would take her if I had her in a hospital or at home. However, they did express a serious concern to a homebirth.

It was Friday evening and I had just had my visit with Jamez. The next day was Valentine's Day and a huge blizzard was beginning to arrive. The next morning, I was fixing breakfast with Thomas but we got into a disagreement and he didn't talk to me for the rest of the day. Meanwhile, I was having contractions that got worse by the end of the day. I had definitely decided on the homebirth recalling the unsettling events of my first birth at the hospital. I knew it was something the Department had warned me against, but I felt very strongly about bringing my second baby into this world in a calming, non-invasive environment. Finally, Thomas came into my apartment as he was squatting in the adjacent apartment next to mine. I asked if he would make me some tea and he got mouthy with me when I requested he fix it a certain way. He said he would fix it the way he intended.

I made myself a warm tub and when the contractions slowed down I got out and went to my couch in the room I had set up for the birth. My couch had a plastic covering and large pads to absorb any blood or fluids. I ended up seeing a pinkish discharge and became concerned especially since I was in so much pain. I knew pain could be an indicator that something wasn't right. I asked Thomas to call an ambulance. He asked if I was sure and I yelled that I was in pain and to do so now!

I was all clenched up, lifting my body with my hands and feet onto the couch. My whining was making me mad so I pulled myself into control and was able to breathe through the pain realizing that the whining wasn't helping at all.

All of a sudden my water broke and I was over the bucket I had on the floor, feeling Ella's head crowning! I yelled to Thomas not to call! Apparently, the yelling did not help because he did not come back right away. When he did *return, it was obvious that he had already called. I tried calling them back, but it was too late, they were already on their way. I actually wasn't even sure if it was Ella's head I was feeling, but asked Thomas to catch her as I crawled back onto my couch. With one push, she was out and Thomas handed her to me! It was the second miracle of birth, and I was so proud to be cuddling my precious newborn in my arms; a moment that a mother never forgets.*

<"Hi Mommy. Thank you for bringing me into this scary world with such gentleness and ease of transition. I really appreciate your concern to make things right for me. I will remember your terror when that knock on the door came. It is that fear that has grown within me and settled in my first chakra. I will love and bond with my foster mother as you and I had planned but she is not you, my birth mother. I will always deeply love you too as I know your warmth. Your sweet face will be stored in my mind's eye. Try hard to stay brave Mommy.">

She was very slippery and I asked Thomas to retrieve the blanket I had prepared as it was across the room. He saw the ambulance arrive and ran downstairs. I rushed across the room to retrieve the blanket myself and blood poured down my legs. I got Ella to latch onto my nipple when Thomas came back. He told me I had to go and talk to the police.

"Come on! I can't go downstairs, I just gave birth! Are you crazy?"

Thomas left and sure enough—"Knock, knock, knock"

"Who is it?" I called out. It was the police of course. I pulled the pad off the couch and slipped it between my legs in a way to hold the blood. I shimmied my legs to the bathroom and threw on my bathrobe covering myself the best I could.

I cracked the door and told them everything was okay, "I just need to tend to my baby" as I bounced Ella in her swaddle. They asked me when she was born and I told them a few days ago. After I closed the door, they knocked again and asked my name and birthdate and had me spell the name. I told them my name was Starre Kadingir born April 24, 1989. Luckily, they left for good this time.

Finally, I was able to relax and birth the placenta. I put the placenta in a plastic bag and closed it up to the cord, keeping it upright. Ella took her thumb and soothed herself, so I was able to put her in the crib and go clean up. Thomas came back and got to hold her for a little bit. After he left, Ella and I slept alone in my bed and we woke up together.

She was awesome! She rested and I was able to make myself some breakfast.

Thomas came in to check on us and cleaned up most of the blood and then he went back to his own apartment.

Suddenly, a knock at the door made my heart skip a beat. I felt the dread wash over me.

"Starre, I'm here to make sure you and the baby are okay," said a voice from the other side of the door.

"Who is it?" I asked.

"It's your case worker."

"You don't sound like her." I went to the door and opened it. There was three or four police officers with her. I sunk even further, but held my cool. I held up the baby to show them she was fine.

The caseworker insisted we go to the hospital. She told me that I didn't need to get her dressed or put a diaper on the baby. A female officer came in to help me get into some pants while I held Ella and the placenta bag. It was extremely cold and mountains of snow had fallen overnight. I held Ella tight as we were escorted out of my home and into the ambulance.

When we arrived at the emergency room, they took Ella from me right away without letting her breastfeed. Everyone swarmed around her doing different things and not telling her or myself what was going on. (Just the scenario I wanted to prevent by home birthing) One of the nurses brought a pacifier and I asked her not to use it, hoping I could breastfeed. They also cut the umbilical cord without my consent or allowing me to be a part of her care.

Ella was then put into police custody and taken to the nursery. The caseworker told me that if I stayed I could continue to breastfeed my baby. That's a no-brainer! Of course I agreed to be admitted. However, I did not get a room and the ability to be with Ella until six hours later!

I was told that Ella was not drinking the milk and vomited what she had swallowed. (I wonder why?) I was finally able to have my baby with me and we were allowed to stay together through the night. The nurse on duty warned me that if I fell asleep with Ella in my bed she would have to report it (so compassionate!) I stayed up almost all night holding her tight, singing to her, talking to her, comforting her and feeding her until the foster mom showed up the next morning.

First she entered the room pretty much in tears. She came over to me and gave me a hug and sadly explained that she didn't know it was going to be like this. She told me that I had no reason to trust her, but that I could. We had a very pleasant conversation. Helen opened up about her birth experiences and how it led her to become a foster mom. Ironically, she told me she never met a good mom like me who had their kids taken. Someone was ordered to come and check on my mental health and it seemed like Helen was having trouble being around me even though I wasn't doing anything but being there for my baby. In hindsight, I assume she was just very uncomfortable with the whole situation. I guess from her point of view she understood my feelings of having my baby taken away, especially knowing she was the taker.

Helen left the room claiming to be getting something for me that I hadn't asked for and when she returned she told me that there was a "code red" on my room due to me being a "flee risk." She was not supposed to leave me alone in the room. Then without warning a nurse came barging in and took Ella right off my breast! She immediately cut off the medical wrist band that linked me to Ella and told me I cannot have contact with the baby.

"I think Starre would prefer that I take the baby," spoke up Helen.

And there I was all alone in my abandonment, feeling abused and devastated. Maybe I should be on a gurney being pushed into a freezer down in the morgue! The death inside of me was overwhelming.

No one came back into my room for over an hour. With no assistance, I took a shower and called the nurse to get my release papers ready. My dear friend Meg came to drive me home. Meg was a tender-hearted soul who would go out of her way to help others. We shared many a cheesesteak sub together.

The next day I got up early and finally found my breast pump. It was discouraging to "pump" as it was very unnatural and against my beliefs. I was able to fill a small container with colostrum. I kept the vial next to my breasts so it would stay the perfect temperature and I laboriously walked in the freezing cold and snowy wonderland to the hospital hoping Ella Rose and Helen were still there. Sadly, I found out that they had gone home. I tried contacting Kris to see if she would pick up the colostrum since I knew she had made plans to visit Helen. She did not find it important to help me out with this.

I then attended my parenting class, met with my attorney (still walking the day after childbirth) and then went back to the hospital to have my medical records released to Laura, my new attorney.

I stopped by the spiritual division to delve into my beliefs with a professional since my beliefs were being questioned in my reunification plan. I know how important it is for me to demonstrate my acceptance of medical intervention.

I got an email from Kris later that week stating that my new baby had a doctor's appointment the very next day. Kris had testified in court that she discussed with me about setting up my own rides. However, Kris knows that in using the transportation system available, I need to give them 48 hours-notice in order to schedule with them. This is the second time a short notice appointment has been bestowed upon me. I have made it known how very important it is for me to attend these appointments. The first time, I was put under tremendous stress. Firstly, due to losing the Christmas funds I had *saved up because I needed to use the money for a taxicab rate of $54. When I got to that appointment, I was held in the taxi for about fifteen minutes because I couldn't find my card to pay. Then I only got to spend ten minutes with my daughter and was not asked if I wanted to hold her. Again, I was so unsure of my parental rights and my confidence was failing. Little did I know that this behavior of my "not asking" to hold my baby was taken by the department and Helen as unloving and uncaring. My intentions of getting a quick breastfeed in were all but annulled. In a cloud of insecurity, I didn't realize that I needed to speak up for what I wanted and I don't like to be invasive as to Helen's comfort level. I had provided an extra bag of breast milk that I gave to Helen. (I later found out that the milk was warm when Helen got home and she discarded it.) I had to walk at this point from Windham in the cold, six days after giving birth.*

"Please help me understand how I can demonstrate to your expectations by practicing accountability? I feel I have been accountable by attending all the classes and sessions put forth by the Department. I have kept my word, made promises, and fulfilled my commitments. On the other hand, I have not heard any commitments or promises even expressed to me in return. Where is the give and take? Based on my experiences with Kris, only my faults have been acknowledged. In fact, false faults have even been articulated based on small truths. For example, Kris had sent out a letter talking about how to feed the children and follow medical recommendation. When I spoke with the HCI supervisor, Darla, we asked the foster mother ▢what-if' questions about feeding for clarification purposes. Kris then stated that I didn't know how to feed my children correctly or follow medical recommendations! And, as I recall vividly Kris directly told me that she could not coordinate getting that colostrum to the baby when she was first born which was recommended in protecting the baby's immunization. So there you have it—'What's good for the goose is not good for the gander!' To further clarify my interactions with Kris, when I have reanalyzed some of the past events, there have been many occasions where Kris has brought up past events to discredit my confidence as a parent."

CHAPTER 16

Some cheer for naïvetés
But can't you tell I know
Aside from pain and struggle
My strength keeps me afloat.

I was once again grief-stricken that Ella had been removed from her loving mother's arms. Their actions were just getting more and more damaging and corrupt in my eyes. Just how much pain were they going to inflict upon my angel. My imagination brought up the vivid image in the painting by Edvard Munsch, "The Scream." The unspeakable horror becomes so real as you stare into that face. The emotion I fear to be in Starre—indescribable grief as she melts into the earth like the witch in "The Wizard of Oz." I didn't really know how much more pain she would be able to withstand before she literally crumbled into decay. I know her decision to home birth was completely insane, exceptionally dangerous, and quite possibly life-threatening. Starre also knew it was wrong, but it was her desire to bring the baby into the world as naturally and peacefully as possible and to avoid the impatience of the hurried doctors. She really believed it was the right thing to do for a child—to ease the transition from the loving, warm, dark, protected womb into the harsh reality of life; to dim the bright lights and unnatural surroundings that are present at a hospital, to limit the prodding and poking immediately after birth. She just went about it in the wrong way. This plan had backfired as many of her recent plans had. There must be some lesson for her to learn, but all we can see is incomprehensible trauma! The Department had quite openly threatened to hijack Ella Rose from their initial awareness of her pregnancy, which really put a lot of stress on Starre. Their limited vision of seeing only black and white has succeeded in wounding five generations of a loving and gentle family. I know in my heart that DHHS' resolutions may not be punishable by karma because they do believe they are doing what is right. Yet I believe it will never be acceptable in God's eyes to persecute another human due to fear of their religious or spiritual beliefs. To paraphrase a famous political philosopher, John Stuart Mill—The assumption of infallibility about a belief implies that one not only feels very sure of their own belief but also attempts to decide for the other person. It is in stifling dissenting opinions in the name of social good that some of the most horrible mistakes in human history have been made. Socrates and Jesus Christ were two illustrious figures put to death for blasphemy because their beliefs were too radical for their times. No authority should decide an issue for all people. To assert that the liberty of opinion is in danger is that in practice people tend to be confident in their own rightness but not justified because people are hurt by silencing potentially true ideas. It may be wrong but the party in authority has a duty to act on their "conscientious conviction" otherwise they would be cowardly not to act on that belief.

Come March, I was finally able to get back to Maine. The state of Maine really has a better handle on the snow thing. Here in Salem, MA, it was still a mess, the streets were almost impossible to navigate and the snow banks were four to five feet high!

We did a little shopping and had lunch at Whole Foods which was just a block away from where Starre lived. Starre couldn't buy hot food with her EBT card, so I bought her a hot chicken burrito loaded with fillings and she bought me a small piece of salmon and a salad.

Amelia was returning to MA for her baby shower later in March. I figured I could retrieve Starre for the event. It was held at the VFW in Saugus. Starre was still pumping breast milk for Ella at the time. I knew it was hard for her to celebrate in Amelia's good fortune, but she never breathed a word of despair.

The hall in which the shower was held was not separated from the bar, so it felt a little awkward to me. Also they didn't seem to have anything to drink, so we had to purchase beverages at the bar. Amelia's mom, Ann had made all the food and she had done a wonderful job. There was salad, chicken wings, pasta dishes and much more. After eating, Starre gave Keeley, Amelia's daughter and her godchild a late birthday present. She had sewn a hooded fleece jacket and matching head band for her! Keeley was Amelia's first born who was now six years old. After that Amelia opened all her gifts and gift cards. We were so happy for Amelia, despite the misfortune my Starre had befallen. Amelia was a true best friend to Starre and I love her like a daughter.

My little cherub had told me about a free yoga class that took place on Saturday mornings from 10–12 a.m. So in April I arrived in Portland donned in my yoga clothes in time to attend. Starre had introduced me to yoga back in 2011 when we were living with her sister, Sunny. It had become a new part of my healthy life routine, as I continued to practice at least three times per week following YouTube videos. We drove to the community center which was actually not far from where Starre had set up home. It was a nice little group of women. The floor was swept, and the yoga mats were placed in a circle that resembled rays of the sun. The instructor's name was Caitlyn. She was a petite athlete with purpose and poise. She had us introduce ourselves, sharing where we were from and how much experience we had with yoga. Most of the women were beginners, but we all connected as one with the divine, becoming centered while we moved through the poses. It proved to be a gratifying way for me to stretch out after the two-hour drive. It was my first time doing yoga with a group of live people.

When the class was over, I took Starre shopping for her birthday. She wanted some material for her sewing projects. We got the material and notions at Joann's Fabric and Craft store. I was introduced to Renys—a "Maine adventure" where Starre picked out curtains and then we went food shopping. We always seemed to run out of time. Back at the apartment, we got the curtains hung and then I headed home.

Our May and June visits were about the same.

Sunny was approved for accompanying Starre to one of the visitations in June! I was a bit jealous that she would be able to meet and hold Ella Rose, but happy that Sunny was getting "on board." Sunny also joined Starre at a doctor's visit for Ella. Kris was grasping at straws to find something wrong with the new infant, so she would have firm evidence for her allegations of Starre's negligence/abuse. First it was an accusation that Ella was bow-legged, then she had a "cone head," which we thought absurd, as an infant's head is quite normally misshapen from the squeeze out of the birth canal. Later she claimed that the baby may have a brain disorder because she seemed to stare with a fixed gaze at nothing in particular. Starre claimed it was her seeing angels, but that was just "delusional" according to anyone from the Department. At any rate the pediatrician found Ella to be perfectly normal at that time. I thought Ella to be absolutely beautiful and graced big baby doll eyes from her great grandma, Bonnie.

The visitation schedule remained the same, and there was still no forward motion whatsoever toward reunification. Starre still found the visitations to be very limiting as to her style of parenting. She felt bullied into following all the rules, it was her desire to enjoy nature—to play in the sand at the beach, splash in the ocean, jump in the fallen leaves and frolic in the snow. She also had a desire to be whimsical and play "make believe" but felt it would add more fuel to the "delusional" tag. It was kind of like being in a straight-jacket watching as life revolved around her.

I had decided to email Darla, the supervisor at the Department. I wanted her to know that despite Starre's somewhat outlandish behavior in the past, which I felt was due to the trauma she had been through, that I was seeing an improvement in Starre's cognitive thinking patterns. I attributed it to her deciding to go back to school and become re-established with society. Darla was short with me and suggested that possibly I had some information from her past that I may be withholding.

It's a funny thing about Darla, her real name is so beautiful, so spiritual. A name that radiates love from beginning to end and yet she denies its very existence.

CHAPTER 17

July came and I had decided to have a small get together for the 4th. I had only invited my Sunny, her friend Gary, and my step mom, Debbie. She and my dad had raised two boys of their own—my half-brothers. We lost my dad in 2012 to congestive heart disease. I had also asked Joe to invite his sisters, but they already had plans. I was setting things up in the front yard, when suddenly Sam appeared.

"SAMMY! I love it, how did you know?" I ran to give him a hug.

"Starre asked me to come. I know she's been robbed of her motherhood and I wanted to be here for her, as well as seeing you and Sunny."

His smile was so infectious, I was psyched. I love my Sammy so much and don't really get to see too much of him since he moved in with his girlfriend. Part of me was apprehensive to invite him because I didn't want to deal with his alcoholism but I was tickled pink for him to be present. It really meant a lot to me that he came. Sober he is a sensitive, considerate and high spirited man, so much fun to be with-so much personality! Although I have to say, I can see his face hardening and I don't like it. He's losing his youthful glow, his tenderness.

"So Sam,"

"When ya getting sober?" He finished my sentence with sarcasm. "You know it is what it is, Mah. I'm planning on being good today though." I knew he would—for me.

When Sunny came I was completely and ecstatically surprised again— Starre jumped out of the car! Sunny had brought her back from Maine the previous day. Both Sunny and Sam had kind of slipped up on the surprise, but the way it went down, they actually pulled it off! It was kind of funny— one of them asked me to get something out of the car on the other side and when I opened that door out popped Starre from under a blanket! Wow, I never expected to have all three of my children together for a whole day, what a joyful blessing.

Joe set up a chair outside to give Sam a haircut and our little five-year-old neighbor—Johnny was amazed at the idea of an outdoor barbershop, so he had his mom call out the window to tell us. Joe said he would cut Johnny's hair too. So down he came and took the seat when Joe was done with Sam's hair. Debbie also showed up which was another delight for me. Sam behaved himself as I know he likes to give me that respect. There was way too much food, but it was all good. Sunny and I enjoyed our home-made sangria, while our male counterparts were entertained with hand-crafted beer. It started to sprinkle a bit, so we donned raincoats and were just as impassioned as if the sun was shining brightly, which it was in our hearts.

Before we knew it, it was time to take the walk to the waterfront to watch the fireworks. It was a double delight that Debbie was going to walk down there with us. She had typically kept her socializing to a minimum.

We got front row seats at the wharf where the Salem ferry departs. I am always enthusiastic for a good firework display, but was a little disappointed that it was so short after starting twenty-five minutes late. Oh well, the only thing that really matters is the company.

When we got back to the house, Debbie said her goodbyes and headed back to Rowley. We made a fire in my fire pit, with the wood that Gary had brought in the back of his truck. We enjoyed S'mores and kept the fire going until about 12:30. I was pooped and ready for bed. What a fantastic holiday—the first of a new tradition.

July 24th was another enjoyable day. I drove to Georgetown early to meet Sunny.

"Hey Marmaloo! Do you want to take my car or yours?"

"I mean, I figured we'd take yours today. I'll drive Tuesday to the FTM."

"That sounds good. Can you grab the homemade sangria off the counter? I have to do my routine with the dogs."

We had planned a special day to visit my mom and Jack at their second home in Cape Neddick, Maine. Sunny packed some more stuff from her garden for her grandparents and then we got on the road. We headed up 95 to Portland to scoop up Starre; this part was a surprise. We couldn't wait to relax and visit with mom and Jack at their cozy cottage in the country where tranquility was the ambiance; an escape from reality.

As we arrived, they came out to greet us with their little white dog Robbie, a Westie. Jack is quite bent over in his posture now, having had somewhat of a tough life. He lost his mom as a teenager, two of his three children and has survived breast cancer. His grandchildren used to call him "Grumpy Jack" but he really has a heart of gold, a gift for gab and both he and my mom are devoutly religious. Jack, in his spiritual nature thanks the Lord every day for all he has—including my mom, although he still struggles with little things as problematic. My mom is an amazing home-maker and neat as a pin. She has a kind and loving heart especially for her family. She is very quiet and self-conscious always poo pooing Jack when he expresses how beautiful she is.

The five of us hugged and kissed. Our hearts were singing! It had been just about a year since they had seen Starre and met little Jamez.

We went straight to the screened-in patio for snacks and drinks. We chatted casually and enjoyed the birds as they visited the various feeders.

My mom is an avid bird watcher. Even the hummingbirds sipped on the nectar from their special feeder. When it came time for a late lunch, Starre, myself and Mom/Grammy brought the food out to the patio, while Sunny and Grampy Jack drove to pick up the lobsters.

My mom is an exquisite cook. Her preparations are always elegant and healthy. Maine lobster was an extraordinary treat. We delighted in every morsel. After eating, we kept the conversation alive. I brought up the "death thing" because I have been concerned at their age and want to make sure their wishes are fulfilled. Emotions ran somewhat amuck, but it was okay. We all just love our Grammy Gail and Grampy Jack to pieces.

After we settled our feelings, Starre, Sunny and I went out into the field to pick the infamous Maine blueberries. Starre was so cute, she actually decided to pick the tiny little wild berries that were further back. She claimed they were sweeter, but she had to work twice as hard as we did picking from the larger bushes that are just over our heads in height. Starre found herself a small step stool to sit on while she picked, but that was just my Starre—doing things outside the lines. When it was time to leave, we were all melancholic. We had once again escaped the harsh realities of life and now we had to drive through the veil and return to the daily grind.

Just a few days later, July 28, 2015 was an extremely memorable FTM. Sunny and I both attended. Starre had arranged the seating so that the members of DHHS sat at one end of the table and all of her supports circled around the other three sides—this should say something in itself about the unbalanced power of the Department. My Starre set out name tags which was very helpful to me since my hearing is somewhat challenged by tinnitus.

The meeting started with Kris reading an update on Jamez and his infant sister, Ella, that had been written up by Helen. Everything was normally appropriate for their ages, except for Ella's spitting up. It felt like they were discrediting Starre, like maybe her breast milk wasn't "good enough."

Next up, Kris and Storm hashed out the extreme crying for Jamez going to and from visits. Kris in her usual negative manner wanted to point a finger that it was any mention of Starre's name that would trigger it. Storm, the GAL, was not trying to place any blame, but he just wanted Starre to know what was happening for Helen. *Do they really not understand?* I thought. He obviously remembers his mom and he now associates her with trauma. It's devastating to realize that he has no way of knowing it wasn't her doing. He's scared, he's been with Helen for a year now; he really doesn't understand what happened; I'm sure he fears for his life.

We spoke candidly with Darla. Darla is a very quiet woman, physically average in height, weight and stature; a bit plain. She has proven to be extremely unyielding in my eyes, it's like she was once tender and gentle inside but at some point had become bitter and filled with fear. In the beginning, Starre had tried to reach out to Darla with Louise Hay's, You Can Heal Your Life. Which basically confirms that what you think about will create your reality. Included is a complete guide to the probable cause of every malfunctioning body part and physical ailment, with a corresponding affirmation for healing. Starre was hoping to help Darla on a deeper level while also giving her insight into the way *her* mind actually worked. You see, Starre believes life can be blissful if the methodologies in that book were practiced. Darla very reluctantly took the book, but outright confessed she would probably not read any of it, claiming she had no time. When asked about it later, Darla had stated that she had thumbed through it but that she had already read many books like it in the past. At this point, I felt Darla's essence to be "rigid," but I held compassion toward her as I thought quite possibly that she was filled with profound sadness and only became that way because of her devotion to her job. The walls she has built around herself are strong. In that same way she seems glued to the Department's doctrine of black and white; metaphysical thinking is too gray an area to accept. Therefore, Starre's unconventional thought process was confirmed as unacceptable in her eyes.

Today, she seemed to be a bit more sensitive toward Starre with her initial statements. She actually gave my typically berated child credit for being smart! It may have been *my* presence or possibly the clinical way to build up a person before tearing them down. Likewise, the tone of the conversation quickly changed and moved to asking Starre if she would consider changing her way of thinking to a more acceptable society norm. Starre told her that she became depressed when she thought about changing her current way of thinking. Darla in turn stated this was the reasoning that she could not consider reunification at this time. I felt defeated right off the bat, my heart literally dropped like a heavy weight right down to the pit of my belly. I couldn't understand Starre's stubbornness to not "work with" the Department on this one front. Although, I did have a chance to turn that around later on. It really isn't right that they expect to control her every thought and action.

Next on the agenda were several support people that Starre had asked to attend to speak on her behalf. Starre had chosen three people: her newest attorney, Laura, her individual counselor, Mia (who also did not agree with the delusional diagnosis), and her "parents as partners" representative—Lyn. Their contributions were all quite exceptionally positive! They, like myself had seen great forward strides. I was quickly restored to a higher state of mind, while it didn't make sense to me that with all this support from respected members of society why DHHS still considered Starre such a "threat" to her own children. The trio presented a glowing review of Starre's continued progress on all accounts.

Next, we heard from the very shy and meek visit monitor who also spoke clearly in favor of Starre.

As an added support, Meg a personal friend also sat in attendance for moral support and positive reinforcement. She was a kind soul, quiet, respectful and forthright. I felt really good about her and her strawberry blonde tenderness.

Starre had reserved some time for me to speak next. I had written a very organized and heartfelt account of how the outside world was viewing the cruelty and unfounded negative actions yielded by the iron hands of DHHS as having destroyed my precious daughter's entire world. At this point, I was feeling so anxious about going through with it, as I was certain that there were no words that could ever bear any leverage in this deeply disturbing situation. I thought to myself, *Feel the fear and go for it anyway.*

I started by saying that I regretted having to *read* my statement, as it would have more impact if I could just speak form the heart, but it was just too long to memorize. I made it clear that I did not mean to point the finger by repeatedly saying "you, you, you," but that it was necessary to portray my thoughts as I felt them. The "you" and "your" in general obviously refers to the Department of Health & Human Services, while the "I," "we," and "us" refers to ALL the relatives from both sides of the family. And so it went:

"Thank you for allowing me time to talk today, as not just a mom but a regular human being. I am hoping to spark just a glimmer of insight into your hearts and minds and to accelerate the stalled reunification process. I know I can talk until I am blue in the face, as my thoughts have been labeled as 'just an opinion.' But, I ask in all honesty, are your thoughts and convictions anything more than an opinion as well?

I know your goal is to 'save' the children and *maybe* someone somewhere thinks you are doing a great job, but in my world it doesn't seem that way at all. I feel you've over-stepped your boundaries and dragged your feet, and now it seems as though you are stumbling. You are deeply hurting, bullying and destroying MY child's life, heart and soul. As a small collective community—DHHS' opinion differs greatly from my own, Starre's and all the relatives of Jamez and Ella, as well as the general public. In fact, if Starre was allowed a jury, she would have her children back. Just so you know, we are mothers, grandmothers, great grandmothers, a great-great grandmother, aunts, uncles, great aunts, great uncles, grandfathers and many, many cousins.

Although it may not be your intention, the result is quite clear to all of us. You are denying us all the right to touch, hold, nourish, teach and truly love our youngest family members. You have denied Starre her birthright of being a mother. She has missed several "firsts" in Jamez' life. She has missed his first steps, his first birthday, holidays and more. Do you have any idea what it is like for us grandparents to observe a small grandchild who turns to his grandma with his arms up and say, 'up nanny' while never knowing if we will be able to experience the same? Or how any of us feel when passing children's clothing racks while out shopping? Or the sadness that washes over us every time we see a mom with a baby carriage? It's truly heart-wrenching.

Do you realize that you all are just a miniature part of society, that there's a great big world out there that shares a different opinion? Maybe, just maybe there is a much bigger picture? While you believe you are "saving two children, you actually have broken their hearts more than once. A newborn was snatched off a mother's breast! This is a crime against humanity! And, Starre has been severely traumatized a well. I have to look at each and every one of you directly in the eye and ask, 'Could you survive the treatment you have rendered upon her? Or would you have given up by now? Committed suicide perhaps? Have you even thought of that? Having a client's blood on your hands? Would you even care?' You have demoralized, bullied, degraded, deprived and berated her to no avail. And still through it all she stands strong *because* of her beliefs.

I have been following your actions and it's always something new that delays the reunification process. After all else fails, now you deem her to be 'crazy' because you do not understand her way of thinking. She is a 'forward thinker' and while that may scare you, most of our famous inventors and philosophers were at first thought of as 'crazy' as well. Does that give you a better perspective? Does that justify her belief system as you put it? I guess there is just nothing else to use at this time. Although, I feel you are still judging her for not having Jamez vaccinated and claiming 'violence' upon the dad but these allegations are simply unfounded. It is a parent's prerogative to decide whether to immunize their child—this is not crazy. All she was asking for was a little further education on the subject so that she could make the right decision. Thinking things through before deciding what to do is not a crime, but an admirable quality in a parent. If you think outside the box for just a moment—if the babies were with Starre and we as relatives were able to be a part of the children's lives, I'm quite certain we would have convinced her to have them vaccinated as the benefits clearly out-weigh the suggested side effects. And, if immunization was truly your concern, then why was Ella taken and not allowed all the benefits of breastfeeding?

Now, to address the birthing of Ella Rose at home. This *was* very risky, but seriously, don't you think you had her backed against a wall? Threatening her through the whole pregnancy to take the baby away. Again, I and most of humanity find that kind of bullying unacceptable and unethical! Maybe you could actually look at the amazing courage and strength she had to actually do something of this caliber just to be able to spend a few precious hours with her newborn before she was whisked away. Yes, her courage is amazing!

You have kept Jamez away from his mom now for over a year. And you have directed Starre to counseling for something that you have done to her. Does that really clear your conscience? Do you really think counseling can heal the huge hole in her heart? Jamez does not even acknowledge Starre as his 'mom' any more, can you imagine how badly that hurts?

The scales of justice are not properly balanced here. Since your *opinions* are directed to the court and the attorney general who all work together—there really is no advocate on Starre's behalf. Even the ombudsman who is supposed to represent her client reports directly back to you and never even contacts Starre to give her any advice or support. Two of her attorneys have given up, knowing they have absolutely no leverage. Everyone she speaks to is questioned by you and forced to give up privileged information. You sneak and spy into her privacy, while expecting her to be forthright and honest. There is no one to check on your decisions. What happened to the 'checks and balances' of the law? And yet, I *still* see Starre remaining strong!

Let it be known, that we *do* know Starre and Jamez will have a giant hurdle to face when he is returned home. We can only hope that his precious little heart is as resilient as you think and he does not lose all faith and trust in society. We all know the detrimental effects this can have on his future. I also want to make sure you know that Starre will have our family's unconditional support throughout that process. I have planned to spend a week with her here in Maine and I have told her that I will continue to come to Maine on the weekends to help with errands and especially food shopping.

Can no one see how Starre has blindly followed your requirements, only to still be unethically punished and shot down over and over. Can you not see her enduring strength and commitment? Her sweetness, kindness, and joy emanating like the glow of an angel while she is being berated and bullied? Never turning to drugs or alcohol for comfort? Aren't those outstanding qualities of a great parent?

In conclusion, I and all of Starre's family feel she has been punished enough. She has used her time wisely, strengthening her parenting skills and has learned many valuable lessons. She is getting stronger and smarter every day. She has attended every meeting, support group and counseling session; made every visitation on her own two feet through all kinds of weather and varying health conditions. She has never lost her temper or shown any signs of anger toward the Department. She has been steady and stable. She has prepared a home to welcome her children. I stand firmly in my belief that she poses no harm, only love for Jamez and Ella Rose. Please, I ask for all of us, return the children to their rightful parent ASAP."

The room remained silent for a moment. Darla sat through the whole thing, listening intently to every word I spoke, unbeknownst to me taking mental notes to completely discredit me from any guardianship or visit monitoring. I mean, my vigilant and overwhelming defense of my daughter only confirms my clouded vision in their perspective. I know I have been emotionally blinded to the realities of the jeopardy order and here I was again exposing my own soul to the discriminating eyes of the law. Kris would not look at me at all and pretended to take notes while beginning to get agitated and turn red. Storm, the GAL, was furiously taking notes while shaking his head over some of the things he felt were not true.

I feel my words may have had a positive impact on Starre's behalf. I believe the Department and the Guardian were ready to start the petition to close the case entirely, but after I spoke, it seemed that Storm may have had second thoughts about Starre being wronged and decided to give her a second chance. He then spoke in response to Starre's visitation requests. He announced moving forward with two longer visits per week with both children, rather than the three visits—one for Jamez, one for Ella, and one with both. In retrospect, I can see that this may have been for the foster mother's convenience and not solely for Starre's benefit.

He also said he would allow outside visits at the park! (Finally). Starre also wanted to be able to hold Jamez at the doctor's appointments. This is when I saw the women—Kris' and Darla' facial expressions change. It looked like, "wow, she does have feelings." Kris even spoke to say, "We were wondering why you never took the initiative to hold him." Somehow, they didn't realize that Starre, not only didn't think she was allowed to but had frozen all her emotions in order to cope. And with all the bullying and putting Starre in her place she actually didn't think she had any rights at all, which in my eyes the department should have realized. I just didn't understand why they worked so closely with the foster mother while Starre was the one that needed more guidance and support—she was the one that had been traumatized beyond imagination. I think she was intentionally left to flounder so that she would have to figure things out on her own. *Her* focus was on the bulleted list of demands instead of proving herself to be a worthy parent. She needed to be *guided* to understanding that she must work on dissolving all the jeopardy claims as well.

Starre also wanted to be able to call Jamez in the evenings to say, "Good night." This was when Kris' irritation flared up as we had seen before. She started with her unprofessional defensiveness and criticism. I can't quite put my finger on it, and maybe it's just impatience but somehow it seems like Starre's case hits too close to home for her. I seriously feel she should be removed, but Darla made it clear that she trusted her judgment on everything.

CHAPTER 18

"There has to be fault found
And fallout for your investigation
To earn its keep."
—Frank Regan *Blue Bloods*
"Guilt by Association"

.

I think it was sometime in August that we found out about Starre's "untimely" third pregnancy! The three of us girls knew that the department would have a field day with this news. Obviously, this showed that Starre was intimate with Thomas at some point in March or early April. Which quite conclusively confirmed the Department's suspicion that Thomas had returned from Ohio at some point, or maybe never left.

"Not sure how I can break this to the Department. I think the timing is essential, so please do not breathe a word about it until I can find a way to let them know," Starre pleaded. "Also, I wanted to let you both know that Thomas has gone back to Cleveland, so at least I have that going for me."

Sunny attended a few of the visitations in August and September, as well as the FTM's. I knew it meant a lot to Starre to have her support. The outside visits were a blessing for Starre. They got to play at the park and go for walks. The beach visits were somewhat disappointing as the children were not allowed to go near the water. Imagine that? The Department couldn't even trust her enough to let the kids dip their toes in the ocean! The unnecessary enforcement of "rules" just seemed to defeat the whole purpose and ruin all the fun.

The home visits had also been approved and it was wonderful to get away from the "room" at HCI. The bond that Starre had with Jamez finally seemed to be reigniting, now that the atmosphere was more relaxed. Starre sent us a video of Jamez waving to Buggy at the end of a visit. "Bye Buggy!" What a sweet little voice. I know it was especially nice for Bonnie and Terry who hadn't seen Jamez since his first Christmas of 2013.

Early in September, on a Saturday, Starre invited me up to accompany her to a Seaweed Festival. It was held on the waterfront, just down the street from the SMCC campus. That was nice because I got to see where she went to school. The festival was free or maybe there was a small fee to get in, I forget. There were a lot of tents set up where you could learn about the health benefits and the harvesting of seaweed. We learned about the different types of seaweed, how the ocean was not depleted of nutrients like the earth is and all the ailments that it cured. We also learned how to cook with it. Seaweed contains all the trace minerals that are vital to our health. We visited booths selling products and giving out samples. There was skin and hair products, as well as fertilizer and food supplements. We watched creative dancing and so much more.

The September 2015 FTM brought about more agony. Just as things finally seemed to be moving toward reunification, Storm (true to his name) announced a motion to "terminate parental rights!" How does this happen when things are going so well? Why do they continue to hold a carrot just in front of Starre's nose, only to take it right away? Is there any end to the cruelty? The unanswered questions will always haunt my tender soul.

Destroying human hearts and souls. The damage has already been done. My feelings that there *never* was any plans for reunification seemed confirmed at this point. How could there be after more than a year? A child's heart is too tender and vulnerable. Poor little Jamez' life had been disrupted at least three times before the department had placed him with Helen. I guess now it's been too long to even think of getting him back to his family as they've denied placement with both Aunt Terry and Sunny. I mean, I do understand that decision but not the soul-level destruction of an adult who's caring, loving, and kind. An adult, a parent, a mom who's been blinded by the lies after feeling she followed all the rules and requirements; a sweet mom who was only able to love and bond with her child for seven months; a gentle mom who went through hell and high water in the only way she knew to keep her baby safe and healthy; a quiet mom who was trying to find a home, who clung to the unattainable love of an unstable man because she truly loved his soul; a man whom she was told had mentally abused her through passive aggression without her realization; a man who was raised with the same deep soul abuse that has now been put upon his own child; a man who was somehow separated from his own mom, now abandons his own child because *his* pain is too deep. Not Starre, she still believes in happy endings. She loves and cherishes Jamez and Ella, they are her whole world, her entire reason for living, for trying to remain strong, while dying inside. She is not willing to give up; this is a parent's first instinct.

I was again deeply troubled and found myself not sleeping for days. One night, I had had enough of the agonizing repetitive thoughts and swiftly rolled back the covers. I jumped out of bed and went downstairs to write a rebuttal knowing full well that it would fall upon deaf ears, as no outside communication was accepted in the court. My virtual tears spilled onto the screen fluidly as words releasing my inner demons.

"Dear Judge,

I understand that you rely solely on the GAL to inform you of what's best for a child's well-being and this is how you make your decision as to their fate. Is this not injustice? There has been a huge miscalculation of judgment and the GAL goes unchecked. He answers to no one.

Meet my sweet, tender loving daughter. She has been wronged and emotionally destroyed. There is no human way to fight the GAL's decision, I blurt out my words of compassion and plead with him, but I feel him bewildered with my unjustified pleading, he knows he has all the power. I thought the whole reason for '"law" was to balance the scales of justice. In the case of Starre Grace Chambers vs. Jamez Thomas Smith there has been severe misjudgment, gross character defamation, betrayal of a mother's love and an unconstitutionally careless and cruel set of decisions.

Here comes the GAL, an attorney by trade enforcing his stretched legalities to discredit Starre. Hiring a psychologist of *his* caliber to deem her delusional, while striving only to assist the foster mother and her quest to adopt Starre's children. This man, the GAL, has used his power to establish the fate of a child that had originally bonded with his mom for seven months by suggesting a life altering motion to terminate her parental rights. Another threat Starre has to live with. This man has only known Starre for a little over a year, during what has been the most traumatizing events of her life. I have known Starre her whole life. I know her to be a person who follows her own guidance, but she is in no way abusive or out-right neglectful. She, herself has been labeled in jeopardy by the courts of Maine. *Everything* that has happened has been an overreaction to a set of events both by the Department and Starre herself. A soft spoken mom who has had her child ripped from her arms cannot emotionally respond to life at this point. Any compassionate psychologist could verify this. Taking a child, not to death, but to be with another "mom" is unforgivable. A mom cannot let go or move beyond at that point, she has been put in limbo with a heart so damaged that she cannot "feel" *anything* anymore. She was weak-ened and did not understand that she had any rights at all. All the counsel-ing ordered by the Department could never heal a destroyed mother-child bond. Although it *has* helped her individual decision-making skills and made her aware of the mental abuse by the father, but will never return what has been taken away.

There appears to be three main objects of truth to the GAL's report of jeopardy on Starre, which I would like to rebut against. In the case of mistakenly staying with the dad who was accused of misconduct and jeopardy may have not been the best choice, but clinging to what's left after a child is taken is a very reasonable response to a broken mother. The parents can both identify with the loss of their child and can comfort each other with that common understanding. Please recognize that the father is completely out of the picture now—he has gone back to Ohio. All threats have been removed and Starre should be able to have her babies returned.

Secondly, it is true that she did not have the children vaccinated, but this is truly a parent's choice and by no means a reason to take a child away. It's also not fair to speculate that she would deny medical treatment in the future because of past actions. It was just following a "well check" when authorities felt obliged to remove the child because she had not consulted a professional regarding his hernia at that point. Yet after three months in foster care Jamez was still untreated! Starre was horrified at a visit as she noticed the bulge had become very large and she reported that something should be done immediately. Starre may believe in natural foods and healing up to a point, but she would never deny traditional medical treatment. She is not a scientologist. Why would she have health insurance if she wasn't going to seek medical care?

Thirdly, it is also true that she went ahead with a home birth after being advised not to. You need to understand that Starre was being threatened throughout the entire pregnancy of her second child. Busying herself with the Department's demands of counseling and meetings and desperate to get her baby back, she waited too long to find a midwife who would assist at home. Or, should I note—a midwife that would risk her reputation knowing that child services was involved. Starre chose to go ahead with the home birth for two reasons—one was that she felt it was a very humane way to bring a child into the world naturally and two—to fulfill her desperate need to have a few hours to hold and croon to her newborn. She did have a pediatrician appointment scheduled for Monday after the birth, but the Department chose to take her new baby right off her nursing breast due to their CODE violations!

Can you discern what is happening emotionally to Starre? The department sets up a psychological evaluation by one of *their* chosen doctors, who obviously follows the Departments' doctrines and supports *their* way of thinking. In this modern world, metaphysical beliefs are a choice and the Department should be able to understand that their outdated mores should not be the sole basis for removing a child. I know I'm not a doctor but I firmly stand against the conclusion that has deemed Starre "delusional." This unjust label is solely another basis for the GAL to move forward with the TPR but seems quite unfair to use, as the ruling is one-sided.

Starre grew up in a very close-knit, average middle-class family. There was no abuse or neglect. We enjoyed hiking or canoeing every weekend, camping every summer. Furthermore, I feel she is firmly grounded in reality, despite maybe having some lofty beliefs of the way life could be amidst the human chaos in our world. She is able to balance work, rest and play; she goes to bed each night and stays awake during the day, she eats very healthy meals, goes to school, keeps her home clean, does her laundry and other basic chores. She has prepared a home for her children and takes care of pets with love and care. She takes care of her own hygiene and that of the children's during visitations. She goes food shopping and anticipates ahead her needs for the upcoming day, packing lunches and water. There is nothing edgy or suspicious about her, she is loving pure and pure.

A DHSS should understand how they have unjustly and cruelly destroyed the well-being of this mother. Since the babies have bonded with their foster family, it would be an emotionally destructive act to sever their loving and trusting hearts once again. But I do think children belong with their rightful mother if she is able to care for them in a healthy and desirable manner. The deception of reunification was an unforgivable farce. If reunification was actually the goal then I feel it would be more appropriate to reintroduce the children for full days, weekends, and holidays rather than the four hours a week that they have now because quite naturally children *are* going to bond with their immediate caretakers after a full year.

Please consider both sides, I know a GAL may hold more respect as to your decision, but if there is any justice in the law, I believe you should see the wrongness of the Departments' decisions as well as Starre's. Two wrongs will never ever make a right. She has been well-educated in parenting and has learned many valuable lessons, something most mothers are never privy to. She has prepared a home and has been anticipating reunification as the Department had promised all along. In favor of the plaintiff, I plead to your heart and humanness to work rapidly but not haste fully toward reunification."

Well, I am able to sleep now, but really wish there could be some outside influence on this situation. Apparently, I find it a little harder to deal with due to my emotional involvement. I do see the Department's stand on things but playing the devil's advocate is the only way to make my point. The thing that eats at me is I know full well that if a jury was involved Starre *would* have her babies.

There are so many, many other parents out there that are terrible at parenting, that are addicted to drugs or alcohol, that expose their children to things they shouldn't, that don't care about what foods they feed them and the list goes on—no one is taking *their* children away.

When DHHS got the official news of Starre's dooming pregnancy, they did not seem too surprised. Her change in dress had only superficially covered up her condition. Their decision on the outcome was not really clear, but we knew that they were not happy about it.

With October approaching, I realized that Jamez' birthday fell on a visitation day. I emailed Kris for permission to attend on October 27th, Jamez' second birthday and Kris okayed it!

I had come to visit and stay overnight on Columbus Day weekend. My daughter and I had dinner in town at a Mexican restaurant.

"I'll order nachos for us to share and for the meal I would like the tacos." Starre had an enormous appetite with this pregnancy as well.

"I'm getting the enchiladas." And so we both gorged ourselves that evening.

Sunday morning Starre made breakfast for us and we did some cleaning. Even with the TPR threatening, Starre insisted to keep moving forward.

"Bummy, I really want to get a toddler bed for Jamez." My eyes raised up at that one, the money issue always seemed to be ignored yet softened with the use of my "pet name."

"I mean, are you sure with all that's going on?"

"Yes, it's important to me. Laura is starting the appeal process and I feel good about it, I refuse to give up."

"Okay then, it will have to be an early Christmas present."

She also wanted a bed frame for herself so she could store some bins under her bed, allowing more room in her bedroom and less clutter. By the time we got back and put the frame together, I really wanted to get home. I felt bad leaving her with the assembly of the cute, red car toddler bed, but it was just getting too late and I didn't want to fall asleep on the long ride home. Starre was also exhausted but had "miles to go" before she could sleep. She wanted to get the bed together and she had homework to finish up. Plus she had been painting the stairway up to her apartment, so she really had her hands full. Somehow she got it all accomplished.

I scored a two-seated carriage from my landlady that her grandkids had out grown. It was a nice Graco. I cleaned it up a bit and brought it with me on the 27th.

I got to Portland around 10:00 a.m. and was supposed to pick Starre up at school, but couldn't figure out the way. After several tries and failures to get to the correct campus, I texted Starre in defeat and close to tears.

"Don't worry, I can see the bus down the street. You can meet me at One Monument Square."

I had been there before and only hoped that my day would turn around and I'd be able to find the way there.

Success! I even found a place to park. I walked out into the square and spent a little time in the sun while reading the engravings on the monument itself. I decided to listen to some voice messages from Sunny that evaporated my stressed out mood. Her light-hearted voice had a way to bring peace to my brain and joy to my heart. I heard the bus arriving so I walked up that way and spied Starre walking confidently with the red baby bump protruding from an unzipped white fleece. I snapped a photo of her before she realized that I was there. She looked so cute in her red and white outfit. When I got up close and hugged her, I was again amazed at how beautiful she was. I looked into her pretty blue eyes and saw how perfectly she had applied her mascara and how soft and smooth her child-like skin was.

We went into CVS so she could get a birthday card for her precious Jamez. Unfortunately, they didn't have the card she had previously seen about a month ago when shopping with her sister.

"I know where there is another CVS. Can you bring me there?"

"I guess so." Figuring it would be another wild goose chase, but they actually had the card she was looking for. It had a little car that lit up and drove around a race track while revving its engine. Another success. We then went for a quick lunch at Whole Foods. Starre bought us some pre-made falafel wraps and fancy juice drinks.

"This is so good!" I savored every bite, as it spoke to my soul on an organic level of goodness!

We hurried back to the apartment to get things ready for the visit. Starre had me bring an extra candle so she could teach Jamez to blow it out. The next thing we knew the foster mom had arrived. Downstairs we went. Helen brought the two children out of her van. I was ready to head right upstairs, but was told that we had to wait for the monitor! Fortunately, she showed up quite promptly but due to Jamez' urging, we walked down the street so he could watch the trucks! He loves trucks (and cars.) There was a construction site just down the street where bulldozers and backhoes were digging and loading dirt into a dump truck.

Ella let me hold her for a while, until she realized who she was with and wanted mommy back. Starre happily took her into her arms and of course Jamez wanted "uppie" too.

Starre didn't mind holding both because of her situation and bonding desire. Although her baby bump was getting quite large, she managed with seemingly no trouble. I know if the children had never left her, she may have handled it differently, most likely telling Jamez that it was too hard for her, or that he was too heavy with her already extra poundage. We could have easily used the new carriage, but it was all good.

Jamez got down to walk back to the apartment and the monitor picked up the rear. Jamez went up the three flights of stairs all by himself and we gathered in the bedroom/playroom. We played for a bit and then had Jamez open his presents. I had got him a xylophone on wheels and showed him how to make a tune with the attached wand. He didn't really engage with me and ended up holding it up like a vacuum. Starre got his attention as he was willing to listen to her so they opened up the card. It had a big "2" on it, and he was mesmerized by the car that zoomed around the racetrack. Then it was time to open the gift from Grampy Joe. It was his favorite—an interactive Elmo!

Starre put Ella in her jumper seat and she was super happy and giggly to jump up and down. Unfortunately there were rules and she was only allowed to stay in it a short time because of a troubling concern to the development of her feet. Later when I spoke with Sunny about this, she enlightened me with what would be Louise Hay's assessment—"She can't stand it!"

Jamez walked into the kitchen while Starre was changing Ella and the monitor jumped up to follow him. I didn't really think much of it.

We all moved into the kitchen to have a snack. Ella sat in the high chair and Jamez at the table with Starre in between. I fed Ella while Starre interacted with Jamez.

After they both had finished, I got the cake ready and lit the candle. I entered from the next room singing "Happy Birthday." Jamez' face lit up when he saw me coming. I held the cake down low enough for him to see. He didn't need any practice blowing out the candle, with one big puff, out it went! We laughed and put the cake on the table for Jamez to admire. I had decorated it with Cookie Monster and Elmo sugar figures and we let him pick one off to eat. Mommy Starre cut the cake and served it with ice cream.

The next thing we knew, it was time for the kids to get ready to leave. Jamez got his own coat off the hook and put it on. He didn't really want to put on his shoes, so we headed down with them in hand.

Helen was outside waiting and a little annoyed that Jamez' shoes weren't on. She took the initiative to put one on while Starre stepped up to tie the other.

When the children drove off, I felt completely empty.

"Mom, I wished *you* had followed Jamez into the kitchen. Didn't you notice the monitor jumping up?" She felt that it was just another little thing the department would use against her. I was shocked for a second time that day! *What the heck?* I thought—the child was not even allowed to walk into a different room alone! I just didn't understand all these rules and they sure had Starre walking on eggshells.

I'm not sure how Starre was able to face this over and over again and be strong enough to keep saying, "Goodbye" to her own children. I cried on the way home. I just wasn't sure I could keep seeing them, never knowing if I would ever be able to be a real Grammy to them. Starre's courage was truly astounding.

In early November, Storm set forth his intentions for the TPR hearing which was to be held in January.

It's been difficult for me to understand the reasoning behind terminating Starre's parental rights. Although after reading a few articles online, it clarifies that it's all just part of the process. I think it also protects the foster family.

It just seems so severe and binding. She will never be able to reverse this ruling if and when it occurs. She has tried to follow all of the guidelines, so why? Unanswered questions sometimes explode in my head like firecrackers. The conversations that have been kept secret, the unspoken reasonings, the wondering of Thomas' past, the quiet ignorance of a young mother.

CHAPTER 19

Love, hope and ideals
Carry my forgiveness
Tolerance could create clogs
What pauses for my foot down
Is the repetitious clause

The next time I saw Starre was Thanksgiving. Sunny had brought her back to Georgetown after the FTM and visitation the Tuesday before. I was told that Jamez asked for me, "Where's Grammy?" Hearing that melted my heart.

Starre had become a bottomless pit when it came to eating which urged Sunny to call.

"Jeez Mom, she has been eating me out of house and home for two days. I'll be glad to leave her at your house come Thursday. She's monopolized the washer and dryer with about six loads of laundry and taken over my tub for hours!"

"Well, I mean, you know how she is. She does take advantage of every situation."

Wednesday was a full moon. The two sisters, Gary, and a couple friends had a releasing ceremony around the fire pit in Sunny's backyard. They all wrote down things that needed to be released on small pieces of paper and then threw them into the fire under the super moon. Sunny later told me that despite her efforts to get her sister to release Thomas, Starre felt she was not ready to let go of him just yet. While that was a bit disappointing to hear, I guess the rest of the celebration was very positive and nourishing on a higher level.

The next morning, Thanksgiving Day, Sunny, Starre, and Gary, set off for Beverly to pick up Sam and then to Salem for our traditional turkey dinner. I was prepared for them to be late as usual, but they came on time! I was still putting together the fruit, nut, cheese, and cracker platter. They all gathered around and began eating faster than I could cut. It was all well and good. Joe joined in and we conversed over Pinot Grigio and Sam Adams. Sam was being good drinking Coke and the pregnant one drank water with lemon and lime slices.

We were awaiting the arrival of Joe's sisters who would be a little late due to Joanne having to work until noon. She is a manager at CVS, they don't get holidays off. In fact, they work her a bit too hard, but she shares some funny stories with us. She is the "wise guy" of the two. Joe's other sister, Tina, is a bit more reserved, but she has a distinct character as well. She loves Elvis and Batman and has tattoos to express that. She came in with a new Star Wars pocketbook and a Batman scarf! Joanne brought me a small cacti in a pot that had a magnet on the flattened back-side and she plopped it ceremoniously on the fridge—that's her style. Tina brought a bottle of Pinot Grigio.

Dinner was ready right on time and everyone pitched in with the table setting and getting all the vegetable in bowls to place onto the table. Joe carved the turkey. We all held hands while a short grace was spoken to bless the meal and our family. It was a harmonious gathering, we laughed a lot over family stories. After indulging our bellies, we rested a bit before having coffee and pie. I had made an apple and pumpkin. Jo and Tina packed theirs to go.

With all three of my children gathered, they felt it would be nice to have their Dad show up. I obliged their request even though it was a bit awkward for Joe and myself. Around 7:30, the crew was ready to depart. Starre decided to go with her dad to visit with his side of the family.

She returned around 9:00, and we went for a short walk around Salem Common as we had been sitting most of the day and wanted to work off a little of the food. We both wanted the fresh air and exercise.

I made up the day bed for Starre in our spare bedroom. We had planned to depart early on Friday. Morning came a bit too abruptly, but we were able to leave just about as planned.

My daughter had been working at a day school for mentally challenged adults one day a week and we were going there to work on some stage stuff for their play. Starre was using her creative talents as well as her gentle compassion to teach music and dancing and it turned into a decision to perform a play! The production was set for December 13th, so there was really only a couple weeks left to finish the costumes, the stage, and rehearsals for a play that Starre had composed herself. Her talent and creativity were articulated with a complete sense of humility. She was patient with her clients and her efforts filled them with pride. Starre had sewn some of the costumes herself, while masks were made of paper mache. The set for the stage was elaborate with full size trees and a waterfall to boot!

The home visits were going well, and the department approved an extended visit on Tuesdays. Starre finished her classes at SMCC on the 21st.

Christmas Eve came with an agonizing blow. Starre was waiting patiently with presents under the tree, the apartment neat and tidy with time to spare when she heard a noise outside. She looked out the window to see the foster mom driving away. She tore downstairs and caught the monitor.

"Please, please! Call Helen back. I forgot the visit was an hour earlier today. I have presents. Please…"

"I'm sorry," she spoke with no compassion at all, "The rules are the rules."

And that was that. A heartbroken Starre stood devastated with tears filling her vacant eyes. The unfortunate carelessness of time had ruined everything.

"Christmas just won't be the same now. Bah Humbug! After Jamez and Ella open their presents with "mommy Helen" and their dad, it will mean nothing to them with me!" Her voice was cracking as the negative thoughts and horror just kept filling her head.

"How could this have happened? I hope it wasn't the distraction of Thomas being back in town."

"No, Mom. I am completely concentrating on my kids! I just passed over the time in the email from Helen, thinking it was the same."

I knew I had heartlessly hit a nerve. She wanted to give up again. Nothing seemed to go right. The FTM gave hope of extended visits and a possible out-of-state visit with their blood relatives. But it was all shot down … No, No, No.

The Department takes an extended visit and puts parameters on it with their rules. Starre never gets to be the mom she wants to be. Now she has to include nap time into her visit. While that may be reasonable if she had the children all day, it just doesn't seem feasible after they have already rested an hour on the trip to see Starre. So she again looks like a fool in the Department's eyes because the children do not want to nap, time with Starre is so short, they want to engage in play. She is merely a glorified babysitter. There is no respect or consideration of the position they have put her in. They want to see rules and proper care followed, but with as little as four hours a week, how is this possible? Now they have more ammunition to revoke her parental rights!

To top things off, the week after Christmas presented with an ice storm which cancelled the Tuesday visitation and Friday's visit was already being skipped due to New Year's Day. And so the year ended on a sour note.

CHAPTER 20

2016

Finally on January 5th Starre was able to spend time with her children. It was only a short visit so they didn't even get to open all the Christmas gifts. It was indeed, as always a refreshingly wonderful visit. The following Friday was the extended visit and the remainder of the presents were opened. Nap time was a bust but everything else went well. The plate sets I got were a hit. Jamez' plate had broken and he loved the "red car" theme with the matching bowl, fork, and spoon. Ella's set was the princess theme which Starre said was perfect. Bonnie had also sent gifts—a water play station, books, and a soft baby doll. Unfortunately, the little snow sled would never be utilized by the real mom and her children.

The three-day hearing for the TPR was set for the following week. This would mean no Friday visitation and also that I wouldn't be able to attend as Joe and I would be on vacation in New Orleans.

One of Starre's associates from the Hour Exchange where she volunteered had become a very dear friend and was planning a baby shower for that weekend following the hearing. Her name was Mary—quite befitting considering the whole situation. Mary was a great friend and support, she gave Starre rides to all the prenatal visits, bringing homemade almond cookies and healthy shakes. True to her name, she took Starre under her wing during this time of great turmoil. Her kindness and generosity were aglow in her planning. While I would be missing the festivities, I *was* able to shop for some gifts the week prior. I went straight to Sunny's to drop them off for her to bring. My husband and I left for New Orleans early Sunday morning.

It was a hugely busy week for Sunny, not only was she testifying at the hearing on Thursday morning and planning to attend the FTM on Friday, but Wednesday was their dad's birthday and she wanted to celebrate with both Starre and Sam. This meant there would be three trips back and forth to Maine.

The three days of the hearing were long and agonizing. Starre felt somewhat positive after first day, the second day left her with a bad taste in her mouth, and the final day ended back on a sour note. She was keeping me updated by phone. All of Starre's supports were able to speak on her behalf and the newest attorney, Laura, had executed a marvelous rebuttal in a more professional, less emotional format than mine. Laura had worked extremely hard to present a report, which to my surprise had hit on a lot of *my* rebuttal comments that were privately written up. I guess, when Starre took the stand on the second day, she agreed to proceed in the manner advised by her attorney, but felt it was ill-fated and likewise did not have the outcome that Starre had envisioned.

Luck was again on my side as the weather caused a reschedule in the shower plans and now I would be able to go!

The following week presented with the normal two visits. The kids got to splash and play with the water park from their great grandma Bonnie. My Starre reiterated a moment where she sensed Ella's sadness for wanting one-on-one time with her mama and Starre was not able to oblige her. She still held the baby's facial expression vividly in her mind and she felt remiss. She also told me of her crazy busy schedule and how it just didn't allow her enough time to get everything she needed done before the third baby was to arrive.

After the FTM on Friday, both Sunny and Starre had tales of woe to share with me.

Saturday was the rescheduled shower plan. This time we were due for a winter storm. Maine, it seemed would be missed as the course was predicted to be coming in from the south. So the baby shower was on! It was a little risky for us in MA because as with any storm it's difficult to predict the exact impact and timeline of arrival. We were due for only one to three inches *unless* it changed course. Although the south was getting hit badly and there were already twenty-three inches in some areas, it was headed out to sea as planned and not due to hit our state until later in the day.

Sunny and I had decided to go for it, we could always leave the shower a bit early if the blizzard decided to accelerate into our area earlier than expected. I had made some vegetable lasagna twirls, kale chips, and a red velvet cake which I loaded into my car.

I got to Sunny's about 9:30. The dogs of course heard me pull up and started in with their greetings. As I squeezed in through the door so as to not let anyone escape, I was greeted with their usual enthusiasm. Sunny put the bag of baby clothes I had dropped off a week earlier up on the counter. I figured that because the Department's decision on the birth was still unknown, that I would try to pull out half of the outfits from my gift bag. I had spent way too much. As I started admiring all the cute outfits, it was extremely difficult to eliminate any. Even Sunny was melting with how adorable they were. She was inspired to offer me half of the money so that we could split the gift! Always the problem solver, she never disappoints. In fact it's kind of funny but one night while we were all sitting around the campfire at Sunny's home in Georgetown, her brother Sam came up with a new acronym, WWSD—"what would Sunny do!" I guess we all rely on her logical mind for guidance. Sunny is able to manifest anything she puts her mind to and has become very respected and admired by almost everyone who gets to know her.

Sunny and I arrived at Starre's with plenty of time to spare. I was even able to help Starre get the infant car seat and bouncer out of her overly packed closet in preparation for the birth before we departed for the festivities.

It was only ten minutes to the party according to the GPS. We were the first to arrive, bringing with us the guest of honor. Mary had the room all decorated and some of the food put out. The other guests started pouring in, no pun intended. Everyone finished putting out the food they had brought and we all grabbed plates filling them with healthy food.

Time for presents. Sunny sat on one side of Starre to record who gave what and collect the trash while I took a seat to the other side to retrieve gifts and pass them to the guest of honor. In the first bag was the cutest little stuffed penguin that danced to the song, "You are my Sunshine." Unbeknownst to all of us, this was Starre's song for the kids. It was silently agonizing but she persevered. There were many practical and thoughtful presents as well as a slew of outrageously adorable outfits.

Afterward, we played a few games organized by Mary. We socialized quite a bit and learned how everyone had come into their own names. It was a very positive experience. Mary who was actually a doula wanted Starre to tell the guests of her plan to birth the baby as a whole, albeit not cutting the umbilical cord. Mary was very proud of Starre's decision to engage in natural childbirth. She sided with us, feeling it was the best way for a child to enter the world. She also emphasized that *everything* Starre had done was for the complete protection of her children. Starre reluctantly took over the conversation and told us of her wishes for a quiet, dimmed light, natural experience with as little clinical interference as would be allowed. She would be assisted by the midwives associated with Mercy hospital; it all seemed acceptable—even the part about letting the placenta birth on its own.

We finished up a bit early which was good because I didn't want to burden anyone else with packing up the gifts and bringing them up the three flights of stairs at Starre's apartment.

The first part of the ride home was spent rehashing the events of the FTM. Sunny, contrary to her nature, was extremely negative. She told me that Storm had told Starre that there was a 90 percent chance that the department would take away the third baby. He told Sunny that Starre's best bet if she wanted to keep the baby was to have Sunny become the guardian. That way Starre could live with her and be with her baby full time. Starre did not want to do that!

"How does that make any sense?!"

"Well honestly, it would mean that Starre would have to leave her apartment and her life in Maine. She would lose her independence and have to move to Georgetown where she wouldn't even have a room of her own. She would be exposing her newborn to the sudden startling eruptions of loud barking and your roomie's disruptively negative oral outbursts, both of which often seem to dissect the otherwise positive and joyful flow of energy. Plus she would have to deal with sisterly competition. Besides, I don't believe you want to be financially responsible for her which would mean her getting a job and a room somewhere close. I don't think she's ready for that—it would make you the full time mom and she would be more like the auntie."

Sunny then brought up the new issue the Department had exposed. GA—General Assistance. GA was the agency in Maine that assisted parents during their transition to self-reliance and had likewise had become the source of Starre's rent and food money. It seemed that the Department felt Starre had been lying to them in order to keep the apartment. This was a violation and punishable by law. She could be arrested and put in jail! Oh boy, it would seem again that I am just too emotionally involved to see the significant lines of the law.

"Of course, they wouldn't want her to have her children if she was going to be put in jail." One more success for the Department.

The thing was that Starre truly believed in the promise of reunification. We both believed the longer visits, the home visits, and the outside visits were working toward that outcome. I guess that was just dangling a carrot in front of her nose so it looked like they had fulfilled their obligation. At this point I think DHHS had decided the children would be better off with the stability of Helen and her husband's home with its unified love and concern.

Sunny just kept on in this manner stating more negative things about her sister and wondering why, when she was willing to put herself into the guardian situation which would be a huge burden to take on, that Starre would not want to work with her. I felt very saddened.

"Okay," I said, "Let's move on to new conversation." As the mother of these two unique personalities, I understood both sides. I suggested more of an interview with Sunny so I could fuel myself with more knowledge for this book. I asked her what she encountered at the doctor's visits she had attended. This didn't work too well either because she was not focused to that extent. At least I extracted the subject matter and why the appointments were actually scheduled in the first place. I made some mental notes and we moved on.

Sunny and I arrived to her place just as the snow was starting to fall. My drive home to Salem was somewhat more challenging. The storm swiftly flew in with near whiteout conditions. I drove very slowly and carefully as befits my personality trait anyway.

That night, Starre called and wanted me to do a flower card reading for the outcome of her situation. I could tell she was extremely emotional and feeling negative as to the Department's decision. It was all residual effects of the previous day's FTM.

Starre told me how she had picked four cards in a spread from her angel oracle cards. First she set out some archangel cards from another deck to watch over and bless the reading. She asked what her lesson was, what needed to be removed or changed, what was influencing the situation and what would be the outcome? She didn't feel satisfied with the answers. I'm sure it was clouded by her emotions, so I told her I would call later with my own results.

I decided to pull three cards from my "Flower Therapy" deck. Concentrating on the situation and praying for guidance, I flipped over three cards. The first one was "First step," hydrangea. It stated that now was a time for transition and breaking down the problem into small steps instead of focusing on the whole would make it easier to handle. The message was very clear to me—this card was a sign that Starre had allowed fear to prevent her from making any progress. I thought it to be referencing her alleged lies and unspoken truths. But it went on to say that it was okay, she is now ready for a change and the angels would support her as she let go of the fear and moved forward toward her bliss. I felt it was confirming that she had made the first step in her final decision to let go of Thomas.

The second card was "take time for yourself," pink tulip. This one was easy and needed no explanation as tomorrow was Sunday her "tub day" and it would be important for her to honor this tradition with extra love for both her and the baby.

The third card came up as "world energy," agapanthus, a flower, I was not too familiar with. I was not happy with this card and decided to sit on it a bit. I finished one of my virtual puzzles which helps relax me. I was still unsatisfied with that third card. I put it back in the deck and reshuffled. Sure enough it was meant to be and came up again! As Doreen Virtue says, "You can't make this stuff up!" I figured I would refer to my "Flower Therapy" book by Doreen Virtue and Robert Reeves. The book was a separate purchase and goes into a little more detail about the flowers. The explanation in the book gave more clarity to the card's message. Balancing world energy, encasing the entire situation with love, releasing addictions (Thomas) and old belief patterns, and granting wishes! This is what the Department had been saying all along. I know that as an Indigo, Starre wants to believe and do things her own way—which would be fine if she wasn't under the scrutinizing eyes of DHHS. The encasing the situation with love was a very strong message to let go of the fear and see only love. This would bring peace and harmony to each person involved. It was meant to provide healing energy in its entirety. The agapanthus is a long-stemmed flower that forms into a round spherical shape, imitating a wand. The description says to imagine yourself as the good witch Glenda in the Wizard of Oz. Take hold of the "wand" and wave it in the air stating your wishes aloud. Its energy works to heal deeply ingrained issues, and beckons the receiver to clear out all of the old belief patterns, every last remnant. All very encouraging to both of us.

I went to bed with a vision of hugging and caressing Darla and sending her unconditional love. I imagined conversing with Storm and convincing him to see the whole picture, suggesting he be aware of possible misjudgments that may have been made and why. Since he is a logical person he understood. The new case worker was a little harder because I hadn't even met her yet. Even though, I visualized holding their hands with Starre in mind and rejoicing the positive aspects instead of dwelling on the bad and moving forward with trust. As I dozed off a message came to me that the Department did not want Starre to leave Portland and they were not actually going to approve Sunny as a guardian. Satisfied, I fell asleep.

In the morning, I was inspired to pick a card from the "Mermaids and Dolphins" deck that I keep by my bedside. The card I picked was "You're being helped." It stated that although we may not see any progress, heaven is working behind the scenes to help us. Another positive card.

Downstairs, I sat at my table in the sun and picked a card from the *Daily Guidance from your Angels*. This deck gave me the card, "Joy." Joy is what I believe to be my "essence." So it felt good right off the bat for both myself and as a message to Starre. Joy is the highest energy of all and combined with love springs from appreciating the gifts in each and every moment. It's a magical sense that everything is possible as it allows you to attract and create your present and future moments at their highest possible levels!

I called Starre to relay my experience. She seemed unconvinced and I didn't want to dwell on her negative emotion any further, so I sent my joy on a spiritual level and we said our goodbyes. I was hoping that it was just the energy of the full moon, as Starre's motto is "I can do it!" In retrospect, due to her situation of having two babies removed and the length of time that had passed since Jamez was first taken, it was certainly understandable for her to feel defeated.

CHAPTER 21

I was part of a miracle today January 29, 2016.
A baby was born,
Birthed into a soft pink blanket
Held by my own two hands.

As it happened, I spoke with my due-any-day pregnant daughter on Thursday, January 28, 2016. While talking with her, I got a message from my angels that tomorrow would be the "day."

Focusing at work, I gathered all my upcoming tasks and put a note on top for my covering co-worker. I felt completely confident about this intuitive instinct.

Starre called me later that evening and told me she was having some contractions.

"Do you think it could just be Braxton-hicks?" she asked.

"Not this far into your pregnancy."

I was unsure if I should head right off to Maine or get some rest first. I decided upon the latter. I had told Starre to call me around 3:00 a.m.

"Dear Angels of mercy, please accept my prayer for a safe birth and carry my wishes gently upon your wings up to God for the greatest good of all involved. So be it."

I had a little trouble falling asleep while pondering over additional items I would need for the trip that I hadn't already packed. I went into a dreamlike sleep where I visualized what I would do when I got the call from my daughter. Falling into a deeper sleep, I slumbered peacefully. Probably about 3:00 a.m., I had a realistic dream. It seemed like I had had this same experience in a former lifetime. In the dream, I woke up and went through the steps I had previously planted in my mind to gather the items I had forgotten to pack. When I was all set, I wheeled my suitcase down a long hall, passing rooms like in a boarding house or college dorm, speaking to those who had their doors open as I went by. Pausing outside the last room on the left, I announced my exciting news, "Today's the day!" There were three girls in the room, they wished me good luck. One of the three appeared to have just arrived and was visiting the other two. She looked at me. Her reddish hair was up in a ponytail and she said, "Oh, aren't you the girl I knew from high school who was kind of spacey?"

She had a familiarity about her that I couldn't put my finger on. I didn't take offense to her words, they made me feel comfortable. I thought of my sister-in-law, Jan, who had described me as a snobby "prep girl" in high school. I just didn't feel like that was true.

When I got to the end of the hallway, it opened up to a large circular room, like a foyer. High above hung a giant chandelier. It was bright, posh, and open. Decorated in white with gold accents. It was divided off by a railing and set down a half-level. There were three short sets of stairs at nine, twelve, and three o'clock. At six o'clock was the main entrance from outside, adorned with colossal-sized doors. The flooring was white marble, each curved stairway was carpeted in a plush gold patterned carpet. At the twelve o'clock area, just off where that set of stairs descended, sat a desk where a woman (who is now my office manager) stood.

"Today's the day!" I exclaimed and she congratulated me and sent me off with her blessing. Another girl that I currently work with also there waiting to speak with the woman in charge.

I suddenly awoke to the text chime from Starre at 3:27 a.m. Contractions were steady at fifteen minutes apart. I jumped from bed and grabbed my suitcase, robe, and slippers from the closet and the clothes that I had set out to wear. Being quiet, so as not to wake my husband, I went down the hall to the bathroom and dressed quickly. I grabbed a blanket I wanted from the front room and went downstairs. I brought the extra things right out to the car. Inside, I opened my bag and packed my makeup and flower therapy angel cards. Zipping up my bag, I remembered that I needed to leave my portion of the rent with Joe. I checked my purse and found the checkbook to be empty of checks. Ugh, I had to go back upstairs into the bedroom and grope around my drawers in the dark to find my checks. Luckily, I found them right away and did not disturb my snoring husband at all.

At 3:43 a.m., I started the car and backed down the driveway.

The drive went smoothly, unencumbered by traffic. I arrived at 5:15. Starre dropped her keys over the porch railing on the third floor. She felt we still had a little time. I got her dishes done and moved a very large cardboard box that she was planning to make into a fort for the kids at the next visitation. Unfortunately, that visitation was today and would be cancelled due to the pending birth.

We arrived at Mercy hospital about 6:00. We were triaged to a small room for monitoring the progression of labor while the room was being readied. Nurse Maura went through the normal intake questions with Starre. She got us both water and a banana for Starre. Mary also arrived as Starre wanted both of us to be a part of her miracle. We didn't get escorted to the room until about 8:30.

The room was quite spacious and accommodating. There was a bathroom just inside to the left. It was complete with a shower, sink, and toilet. A sliding curtain divided the room so as to promote privacy if the door was open. Inside the main part of the room, on the other side of the bathroom nestled in a corner was an ample-sized triangular Jacuzzi. A rocking chair, an upholstered chair, a couch that opened to a bed, a closet, the main bed, and several cabinets filled the rest of the space.

The two nurses, Joy and Jackie, were on the right getting their monitoring station set up. It was all enclosed in wooden cabinets. Pretty posh for a hospital.

Starre handed out some protocols she had printed up to let the nurses know her desire to have as little intervention as possible during labor and delivery. She expected everything to be tranquil and natural.

Starre then gave Mary and myself an affirmation list to read as the labor progressed.

"Mary, would you be able to set the vaporizer up?"

How's that for being prepared! Starre had even packed her own adult diapers to use instead of the hospital pads, as they offered more protection.

The doctor came in to introduce herself and was congenial with the proposed plan.

My little seamstress had sewn several items for the occasion—a birthing outfit for herself, a blanket to catch the newborn in, a placenta bag, a placenta cord wrap, and a newborn outfit all made of the softest pink fleece she could find. The humidifier began to steam which was a big help because the hospital was so dry; great forethought from Starre. Her lap top was plugged in and set to soft, comforting music with a video shuffle of Starre's nature photos.

Labor was progressing unremarkably and Starre was breathing through each contraction while Mary and I took turns reading the affirmations. We could tell the contractions were becoming more intense around 10:45, but Starre still remained dignified and silent. About 11:00, Starre quickly took off her clothes and donned the soft pink birthing outfit she had designed for her birthing experience. She looked so cute, I took a picture of her. We didn't realize that the actual birth was so close because of Starre's silent demeanor. Finally about 11:30, Starre turned over onto her knees with her arms atop the head of the bed that was raised to a 75 degree angle. Almost like a spread eagle prayer position. The shriek came without warning to alert the nurse to call the doctor—"It's time!"

"Get the blanket, Mom!"

I grabbed the pink blanket and got close, I could see the head crowning! What an experience to be on the other end of a birth. I was both humbled and proud. I placed my hands with the blanket gently resting atop under Starre's behind.

Starre reached her hand down, feeling the emerging head. "She's coming!" Another big push and the head emerged! I maneuvered the blanket further under the head.

"I got you baby girl!!" Starre sweetly spoke to Zoe with endearment as she cradled the head in her hand. Those four words will forever reverberate in my mind, as one of those moments in time that will never be erased; the picture of my own daughter with my grandbaby's head in her hand while emerging from the birth canal remains etched in my mind's eye as the dearest memory I will ever have. (At least as amazing as the births of my own three children).

<"Hi Mommy. I love you so much. I know how much care you put into my growth and my birth. It is for us to be brave. I want to be with my brother and sister and so you know I must leave you too. I'm so sorry, I can't even imagine how hard this is for you. I will be raised by a stable family with a lot of love and a good mix of diverse experiences to guide me through life. Thank you for all the centeredness you have given me.">

At this point, the doctor arrived and quickly took action. She had to intervene to help the shoulders out because they seemed stuck. Once the shoulders were through the infant shot out and into the blanket I was supporting. The doctor grabbed the rubbery umbilical cord and pulled it over the child's head.

Starre turned around carefully raising her leg over the baby and the cord to a relaxed seated position. I passed the baby to the nurse who set her into Starre's embracing arms.

The doctor really wanted to pull the placenta out. Starre gently spoke up, "Please don't pull. The placenta will birth naturally within the next ten minutes." I don't think the doctor liked that at all. First off, she must have felt that Starre was telling her how to do her job and secondly, I think that she just wanted to have the whole process be done as quickly as possible so she could move on to other things. No one seemed to want to stay in our room for too long, I think they all knew what was coming.

"I'm just helping it along," she told Starre. "You're bleeding," she tried to use as an excuse to hurry it along. This was against Starre's wishes. The doctor kept pulling on the cord and pressing on her stomach. It was quite painful as Starre tried to hold back her groans. The doctor got her way and the placenta popped out.

I got the placenta bag Starre had made, lined with a zip-lock baggie and covered with the same plush pink fleece that the blanket was made from. The doctor dropped the placenta into the bag. There was a bit of a verbal melee about the Pitocin shot the doctor wanted to give Starre. Starre didn't want it, but the doctor insisted that she needed it and it would help with the bleeding and shrinking of the uterus. That made sense so Starre succumbed and the shot was administered into her thigh with a loud scream from the pain she wasn't expecting.

The doctor was done with her part and she immediately exited the birthing room.

I was actually a little surprised about the doctor's abruptness. It seemed as though it was her pulling on the placenta that had caused the heavy bleeding and usually before a shot is given the doctor explains where the needle will be going in and warns about the pain.

All was quiet for the next hour while Zoe latched onto the nipple and rested on her mama skin to skin.

The pediatrician arrived next. She needed to take the baby to the warmer to give her a physical exam and administer the vitamin K shot as well as the Erythromycin for her eyes. Starre had already approved the medications for the baby. Starre asked if she could carry the baby to the warmer. The pediatrician said, "No." It was not allowed because Starre could become dizzy from the blood loss and pass out or drop the baby, it just wasn't safe. Again, this doctor's impatience was upsetting, she didn't want to take the time to answer any of Starre's questions or come up with a mutual solution that would make them both happy. I was a quite put off by the attitudes of these caregivers. There seemed to be no compassion at all and the hurriedness didn't fit with the sign in the bathroom that stated something to the effect of, "we want our patients to be actively involved in their care."

I grabbed a gown for Starre and got one arm in when the baby got whisked up and brought to the warmer with the placenta bag attached. Zoe, startled at the sudden movement and exposure started crying. Starre flew off the bed to be at her side while I was still trying to get the gown over her naked backside. As soon as Starre reached Zoe, she held her flailing hands and spoke softly, letting her know her mama was still with her and would keep her safe, Zoe quieted right down. The doctor went on with the exam. Zoe was then moved to the scales where she was weighed and measured for length and head circumference. The stats were in—baby girl Zoe was born at 11:37 a.m. January 29, 2016. She weighed 8 pounds, 1 ounce and measured 19 ½ inches.

The natural process of birth was truly a miracle and I had not only witnessed it but had taken an active part as a participant, not a mom giving birth myself. I was so proud that Starre had allowed me the privilege of this experience.

Starre checked in with the social worker as they had asked because they wanted to assess the baby as soon as it was born. We still had some obstacles to face. She asked them to wait two hours as she and the baby were being actively monitored every fifteen minutes to make sure all was okay.

When no one showed, Starre got worried that the social worker had not sent out the email to the "team." She decided to send out her own. The GAL gave her a congratulations and told her she was not involved with this baby unless a petition was filed.

We felt we had escaped the worst scenario. I celebrated. Mary was reassured as well. We all felt at ease.

The department closed at four o'clock so all definitely looked good. Starre sent me home to feed Buggy and when I got back, Mary left.

The nurse announced over the intercom that Meg was here to visit.

"Yes, she can come in," Starre answered. We were both happy to see Meg. Hugs all around. I started to tell her how awesome Starre was in labor—dignified and graceful right up to the first push when the only scream that had escaped her lips was to alert the nurses that the baby was coming and it was time to call the doctor. I told her proudly how I had caught the baby; I was the very first person to hold the newly born precious bundle of joy! I started showing Meg the few pictures I had taken.

All of a sudden with no announcement, in walked Darla and a black girl followed by the two nurses. I froze as she asked Starre to let the nurse take the baby away. Starre wasn't budging.

"Do you have a petition?"

"Yes."

"You can say what you want while I hold the baby."

Darla was not happy. She insisted they needed to have a serious conversation and the baby needed to be removed. She also told Meg that she needed to leave and would not be allowed to visit! Another shock wave surged through me with this vindictive action. Why would Starre be denied friendship, support, and love after they had devastated her for a third time?

After she had followed all the recommendations! They were pushing her to fail, this was *very* clear.

"Nope," Starre reiterated while shaking her head. "I've been through this before, you can say whatever you need to say."

I asked to see the petition. There was four pages of legal jargon before I found the actual petition charges. I read the first sentence and was appalled. It was stating that Starre was a "flight risk" because she had wheeled in the car seat upon admission. It seemed they had interviewed Nurse Jackie over the phone and somehow that had been brought up. As we know, Starre was just being prepared and wanted it to be easier for me to pile up the carriage/car seat with all her belongings so I could make it in one trip. It seemed the nurse had told the social worker that it was very unusual for a mother-to-be to bring in the car seat upon admission. It was typically brought in when the mother and baby were discharged.

I spoke right up at this and tried to explain. Darla was furious, but controlled orally. Physically, her face started twitching like crazy, which is normal for her when she's put on the spot. I haven't figured out why this happens with her, I know it means she's uncomfortable, and I have to wonder why she's never heeded the internal message that it portrays. I've never seen anyone with this much fear of who they are.

"I will not discuss the petition with you," she spoke sternly. "This is not the time and nothing you say is going to change this action right now."

I was nauseated but realized immediately that this was real and nothing I said could deter the outcome. I remained silent while staring at her with dagger eyes. As I skimmed the rest of the petition, I could only shake my head at the outright lies and pure speculation brought forth. I knew that Darla had gone out of her way to get this petition typed up and signed by the judge, disturbing him at home after hours. I was filled with unanswered anger, visualizing myself up close with Darla looking straight into her eyes and giving her a shake. It appalled me that she would barge in here and remove a newborn from her rightful mother directly from the birthing bed with no warning at all.

"What is wrong with you?" I questioned softly and with complete control. My face was both concerned and in wonderment of her vicious attack on Starre and Zoe who belonged skin to skin with her mother.

I got up and hugged Starre with a tearful face.

And so they removed baby number three, leaving us shocked and empty. There are just no words at this point that could comfort or console our longings.

CHAPTER 22

The days that followed were difficult. The Department had acted in haste, and it was amazing that they could veer away from all the recommendations of the hospital staff once they took control. I guess they have their own set of rules. They immediately bathed Zoe which was not supposed to happen for 24 hours according to the pediatrician. The umbilical cord was removed which seemed like another strike against Starre's constitutional rights. I guess all bets are off once the department takes over guardianship. Thirdly, the baby was set to be discharged the very next morning when the hospital wanted to keep both baby and mama until Sunday which was two more days. If Starre had done even one of those things it would have been labeled as "jeopardy!"

Meg left speechless, as she was not welcome according to DHHS. Also Mary had somehow been contacted and told to stay away too!

Joy, the nurse who was present through the whole labor and birth came back with the placenta in a new Zip-lock baggie enclosed in a plastic container with ice. This nurse was the only one with any compassion in her soul. She was very kind and took caution with her words and actions.

A little later, a shift change must have taken place and a new nurse abruptly marched in with a very unprofessional, degrading attitude toward Starre. Obviously, she had been poisoned like the rest of the staff as to

Starre's character. She ordered me to remove the placenta immediately, as it was unsanitary and would smell.

It was decided that Starre would be able to nurse the baby, so she asked for a few minutes to wash up. She called for the nurse to come back. In she walked with a wheelchair as Starre had requested.

I decided to go to bed. I converted the couch to a bed and not that I could sleep, I laid down, my head filled with racing thoughts.

I heard the nurse come back in, but I didn't acknowledge her at all, I was horrified by her attitude. She changed up the linens on the birthing bed and then left.

I didn't know the exchange that had taken place while Starre was nursing Zoe but when the nurse returned with Starre in the wheelchair her attitude had changed some. She even put a pillow at the end of the couch for me and covered me with an extra blanket.

Once she had left, I sat up to talk with my daughter. She told me how she was only allowed twenty minutes to nurse in a locked room with Helen and the nurse. I guess Helen had arrived at some point. Starre said that Helen was incessantly talking with the nurse about Starre's two other children, as she had done before, completely mindless of Starre's feelings. It was probably a nervous conversation that was uplifting to her considering the situation. We talked a little longer and once we both lay down and the lights were off, I found slumber rather quickly. It had been a very long day.

As if adding insult to injury a promised 3:00 a.m. feeding had never taken place nor the 6:00 a.m.

Around 7:00, the alternate nurse from the day before, Jackie returned and Starre actually asked her name because she conveniently had her name tag turned around. I was shocked that she would dare to show her face after what she had done. In my assessment of her it seemed she was a bit guarded, not really knowing how Starre would react to her. I was on my way out for coffee, when I paused to ask her if she had read the petition. She replied, "No."

Starre asked me to show it to her.

I tried to be gentle, "This clearly shows that it was *your* conversation with the social worker that's responsible for the content of this petition. I'm not sure if you are being implicated with lies, or whether these are your actual words, because this is *not* how it happened." Jackie, unashamed confirmed that those *were* her words.

I left the room and stopped at the nurse's desk to let them know I was going down to the café for coffee and would be right back up. I had felt they were a little rude to me the day before in letting me back in, so I wanted to give them a heads up as to my intentions. When I got downstairs, I found out the café was actually closed on weekends. Well, that's a kick in the face, I guess they didn't want to share that with me. That was outright rude! So I returned empty handed, only to be question again upon entering the maternity floor! I put my hand up and with a disgusted look on my face to let them know I was disgruntled, "I guess the café is closed on weekends." They had no response at all.

Upon entering Starre's room, I saw that Jackie was still there and I grabbed the petition from her. Starre had another question regarding her statement in the petition saying she was concerned with the care Starre was giving the baby. I didn't think she answered this question directly, but she did seem to have softened a little at this point and the conversation was shifted to what she had come in for. Jackie professionally went through all the postpartum instructions, counseling suggestions and pumping schedule suggestions. It was determined that we would leave once the baby had left.

Finally at 9:30, a nurse came in with the wheelchair for Starre again to go to a locked room to breastfeed. At that point, I decided to go out for some breakfast since the hospital charged guests $10.00 for anything ordered.

Upon my return, I began to pack things up for discharge. When I had finished, the nurse came in to let Starre know it was time to say goodbye. I sat down to wait, but was elated when I was invited to join. I jumped right up and followed to the locked room. Helen was escorted into the room with the baby all dressed and snuggly strapped into the car seat for departure. I knew this was due to the fact that Starre was felt to be a "flee risk" but it was so disappointing to not be able to pick her up to cuddle and kiss her "goodbye."

Zoe looked adorable and I cooed and spoke gently to her with held back tears. I wished I had brought my phone for pictures. The Starre said her goodbyes as well. We were then escorted out past Helen and Zoe. My and Starre's sadness was overwhelming and we let the tears fall gently down our faces.

We walked back to an empty room. I packed up the carriage/car seat with Starre's belongings. It was overloaded as I wheeled it down the hallway in front of Starre. Not one of the staff said goodbye, they just turned their heads to ignore us. Once we got to the foyer, Jackie thought I should go get the car and pull it up to the drop off/pick up area.

Jackie waited inside with Starre in the wheelchair. When bringing my car around, I entered the "express service" area only to find out there was no access to the pick-up area. I went back around and found the correct way to get to the area to pick up Starre. Laughing at my error, I figured that my confusion would confirm the unprecedented conjecture of our "flight" plans. But that point is moot, so it hardly matters.

My daughter and I were vacant emotionally. Starre had thought maybe a trip to the beach would be nice. We weren't sure how to shed our negative thoughts. Deciding that it may be too cold and windy at the beach, it didn't alter her feelings about not wanting to go straight back to her apartment. She knew the emptiness she would be facing once there. I reminded her that we needed to pick up some food and some medicine for Buggy's tapeworm problem.

After our stops, Starre was ready to return home. She laid down to rest while I did some cleaning and made dinner. We enjoyed salads topped with herb-crusted baked chicken. Afterwards, we sat in the bedroom and tried to do some metaphysical healing with our angels. Starre put the flea medicine onto the back of Buggy's neck, as she told me the tapeworm was caused by her eating fleas. Starre then put the antibiotic into Buggy's food and we went to bed emotionally exhausted.

When Sunday came we took care of things at home. I was gladdened for the free time which I used to employ my nimble fingers over the keyboard recreating our somber moods into vivid imagery on my iPad. The most recent devastation had become a valuable source of substance filling page after page without much effort. The two of us tried to relax as Monday was planned with a full schedule.

Awakening, we dressed, ate, and entered our day with apprehension. Attending counseling with Mia, we were joined by Lyn, the parent as partners gal. Mia was roughly my age I believe with soft blonde shoulder length hair and a natural glow of beauty. She was physically thin but fit and casually but neatly dressed in jeans and a western style shirt. I felt her essence to be "honest and compassionate." My tears were shed sparingly while Mia gently guided Starre in furthering her plan of action while trying to get her to emote. Lyn was amazingly fresh and uplifting. Her dark wavy hair hung loosely over her shoulders. She was curvy and sexy; bubbly, energetic, sensitive, and forward. The hour was over rather quickly and we were off for the laundromat.

After that we met Mary for lunch, picked up the laundry and went straight to the attorney's office. This is where I got to meet the unlikely attorney. Laura was plain, no makeup. She was not too tall but lanky just as well. Her brown hair was straight, not styled but draped behind her ears as she tried to hurriedly munch down an oversized sandwich in her limited time frame. After discussion of the course of action Starre needed to pursue, it was decided that she would forward the entire caseload to a new attorney who could appeal the decision on Zoe with fresh eyes.

I was a little bewildered as I sensed that although Laura had worked extremely hard and put in many hours of her own time into Starre's case, it was evident to me that she did not actually "believe" in Starre. I felt a bit disappointed. It was now 5:20 and Starre had scheduled a chiropractic visit as her back had been bothering her. Finally we went home and had dinner.

Tuesday began with a thorough cleaning to prepare for the visitation.

The visit was fantastic! I bonded with Jamez for the first time and he was amazing. I found him to be very curious and expressive. He talked non-stop and we engaged in lots of learning games. We looked at books and vocalized animal sounds while I acted out animal behaviors having Jamez guess what I was. Ella, who had been quite shy with me was softening a bit, but still quite clingy to her mom who had Zoe in a front carrier. I felt that Ella's essence was more cautious, kind of like her Aunt Sunny; you had to earn their love and friendship through respect.

Starre had to follow a strict schedule administered by the foster mom. Next on the agenda was lunch then naps. I left Starre alone to manage story time and putting the kids to bed. Ella cried the whole time which was not taken too well by Starre. Unfortunately, she had to comply with Helen's wishes as Helen complained that the ride home was unmanageable if the children hadn't rested. Starre would've never allowed that kind of crying to continue for so long, but again she was afraid to listen to her own instincts to pick up her baby and rock her to sleep in her own bed. Finally about 12:30, Starre gave up and we again engaged the kids in play and then snack time.

Meanwhile, I had scheduled a windshield replacement because the small crack that I had in my windshield had grown to over a foot long during yesterday's excursions. Metaphysically, it was reflecting to me that our lives or maybe just our vision was severely "cracked." I met the guy downstairs at my car. When it was done I had to wait a half hour before driving for the adhesive to set.

We decided it would be best to eat dinner before embarking on my trip home.

We went for Chinese food nearby. Afterwards, I had anticipated just dropping Starre off and heading home, as I was truly exhausted from all the physical work of cleaning and lugging stuff up and down the three flights of stairs in the past five days. But, "No," I still had to gather all the trash and recycling and put it out on the street for collection. Oh well, I hugged and kissed Starre goodbye and made my way downstairs with yet another big load.

CHAPTER 23

How-many-times, rings the repeat?
Before I get the task—
When each time seems different,
A new lesson

I had visited Starre on the last Saturday in February. We had some lunch and started organizing one of her large closets. She went to the kitchen to pump her breastmilk for Zoe, while I continued in the closet. I kind of checked in with her a few times to ask her which pile certain items of clothing were to be put in. Suddenly, it seemed when I had finished folding everything, she was going to finish the rest by herself. She opened her arms to hug me good bye. I went with it, although quite perplexed. As soon as I walked out the door, it dawned on me that she was hooking up with Thomas. I texted her on Sunday trying to persuade her from "stumbling." She admitted I was right.

Sunny and I drove to Maine February 26th for what was *my* last FTM. I was prepared to ask the Department two questions. We arrived simultaneously as Starre and Mia, a concerned friend and counselor.

The meeting began with an update from the visit monitor, Shannon through speaker phone. Starre listened and made her own points in response. I was able to get in my first question which was, "Why was the TPR filed so abruptly just after Starre had complied with the last obstacle, allowing the children to be vaccinated?" (The pediatrician had finally gotten through to her about the positive benefits of vaccines.) The GAL just kind of stared at me in bewilderment when Darla and Starre started hashing out the events as to her decision that seemingly had been entirely ignored as a new resolution to the jeopardy filed on Starre. Once that was cleared up, Darla finally understood that Starre *had* changed her mind, before the filing of the TPR. Starre also brought up the fact that every time she had told the truth it was used against her. She was finally speaking up for herself. I also was able to state my opinion about why Starre was able to keep the assistance from GA; that it was not by deception, but because of the "promise of reunification." Starre then passed forward the diaper voucher showing that GA was still supporting her and the visitations with Zoe. It was kind of putting it back in the Department's face.

After that there was a huge melee between Laura, Darla and the new case worker. Finally, Lyn whistled and called a time out as she put the department's lie about already administering the vaccinations right out in the open! (I was shocked!)

I later found out that there was actually a miscommunication between the Department and Helen as she was never actually told to go forward with the vaccinations and she was strictly following the rules.

The next order of business was up and Mia announced that she did not want to be a liaison between Starre and the Department any more. The Department had actually discredited her. She was more concerned with Starre's healing and wanted to move forward with complete trust as her personal counselor.

Storm announced that there would only be two more visits with Jamez and Ella.

The attorney spoke of getting a new CODE evaluation, but was unsure whether the results would be any different. That also confirmed my feelings that she did not believe in Starre and what she stood for. The whole meeting seemed like a fiasco as Darla brought up the speculation of Starre "not giving the children medical care" as quoted in the petition—I spoke right up shaking my head in disbelief and asked Storm if I could call him. He passed down his business card.

Then Darla asked if Starre had had any contact with Thomas. She started in with her evasion tactics, stating it was irrelevant and if he *was* around, well the Department would already know. Suddenly, Meg spoke, "Did you see him? Did you?" Starre was thrown, as she knew she had been dishonest to her friend by omission. Her evasion had worked until that moment and now Darla wanted a direct answer. Starre lied, "No."

"That was my question." Darla responded.

It was then and there that I looked into Darla's eyes and realized her valuable insight into this devastating journey. Her warranted distrust of Starre and knowingness of the truth had possibly darkened her integrity at times but illuminated her insight into seeing falsities that had caused enough hesitation as to Starre's inner motivation.

The meeting was adjourned. Most of the attendees left immediately. I was a bit dismayed that the new social worker did not speak to me at all. She presented as emotionally removed and was more of an observer than a participant.

Mia, Lyn, Meg, Starre, Sunny and I remained to converse. I hugged Lyn for her effort to expose the Department in their own lies. As we walked out to our cars, I sensed that Meg was ready to break into tears. I surmise that she had an intuition of Starre's lie about not seeing Thomas.

Back at the apartment, we had a fun filled visitation with all three children. Sunny and I both got to croon with the precious newborn and watch in amazement as she uttered quiet syllables in an effort to imitate speech. The two older kids rambunctiously played in the giant box Starre had designed as a club house. We played peek-a-boo through the windows. Ella Rose had finally softened up to me and did not run back to Mommy when I interacted with her. After snack, Starre put on some music and we all danced, then we let them bounce on the bed. Jamez and Ella were giggling up a storm. I'm really gonna miss them.

Starre became very depressed and even suicidal for a short period. She went back with Thomas in her despair which probably worsened the scenario, but I empathized with her reasoning. Her life was entirely hollow and echoed with worthlessness.

I did get to connect with the GAL, "Storm, I really feel the petition was filled with untruths. How could they use speculation to take the third child away after Starre had competed all she was court ordered to do? She has proven she's not a flee risk—she loves it here in Portland; she has a home, connects with the community and even attends school. It's also not fair to use conjecture to state that she won't give the children medical care." I told him what actually happened when the pediatrician came in to do the exam on Zoe, and that I thought it was pretty low to ridicule Starre for bringing in adult diapers. I went on to tell him of her preparedness and that she was not telling the doctors how to do their jobs but merely had questions to which neither of the docs wanted to answer.

"I haven't put too much emphasis on that petition. It's more about the fact that we haven't deemed Starre to be a fit parent."

"What? In twenty months the investigation has not been completed? Then why wouldn't Darla have enough integrity to simply state the truth in that petition?" I suppose I knew the answer—it would make her look bad because she and the Department had failed to complete their job.

By mid-March of 2016, Jamez and Ella were no longer able to see or receive calls from their mom. The TPR for Zoe was also filed. Visitations with Zoe continued for about seven months, many of which Sunny was able to attend at but they were held at HCI again due to Thomas being back in Starre's life. The appeal for the TPR regarding Zoe would also be worked on.

Starre enrolled in more courses at SMCC to keep her spirit alive. I continued to visit monthly, in fact in July we had a fantastic day at the Desert of Maine where we took a tour, a hike, and visited the museum and the butterfly house. Then we had lunch in Freeport and went for a swim at a beach.

Come September 1st, Starre melted into the abyss of homelessness as she had to leave her apartment for renovations and could not rely on GA any longer as she was childless.

The Departments' bullying had convinced her that she was not a fit parent. I let her be on her own to stretch and grow and to somehow, hopefully find the silver lining and lesson of her experience; although we still do not know what that is. I do know that it is only through pain and suffering that we can ultimately find hope. As time goes on and we see the level of care and love that Helen and her husband have for the children, I can only feel that Starre has graciously given the most precious gift that anyone can offer—that of human life, her own children. And we do have to feel blessed that Helen opened her heart and her home to all three, honoring the sibling bond.

There is no further contact for Starre. Her days are saddened and filled with longing. She called me with the final determination of the appeal regarding Zoe. One of the stipulations remaining to the jeopardy that Starre had to conquer was the fact that because she did not want to take medication, the Department felt she was not seeking proper treatment. Starre found a reputable doctor at The Maine Medical center who monitored her for a couple months and agreed that medication was not what she needed. The doctor felt that Starre was emotionally very strong *due* to her beliefs that had been previously frowned upon. However, her documentation did not reach the court in time for her to testify at the final appeal. In Starre's opinion, the new attorney that Laura had asked to take over the case did not seem clear on what needed to be proven to reverse the TPR. She, the attorney also did not seem to think that Starre had enough legal knowledge of the issues to work more directly with her *and* she continued singing the tune that Starre was still totally against vaccines. Starre had wished that Laura had stayed on for the appeal as *she* knew the case like the back of her hand. At that point, both the "flight risk" and the "vaccination" factors *had* been resolved but the attorney did not use those considerations. On March 2nd, 2017 the finalized TPR on Zoe was filed. The four deciding factors were:

1. Starre had not been treating her illness.

2. Failure to leave the punitive father before the proceedings were held.

3. Homelessness.

4. Admission from Starre that she was currently incapable to care for her child.

It's dismaying that when I looked back at the original jeopardy order and the nine point court ordered list, I found that Starre had made amends on all accounts except her relationship with Thomas. Starre's on-and-off again relationship with him has left her untrustworthy with DHHS.

I want it understood that it's my belief that dads are extremely important to a child's development, regardless of his condition. These were his children and they needed him as much as me for supporting who they are and where they come from. I am not the only one with a broken heart!

I have to agree with Starre, Thomas was never given any rights, he was completely disregarded because no one wanted to take the time to understand him.

There are several reasons to file a TPR. The one fact that is solid is that the children have developed a strong and healthy relationship with their foster family. The sole remaining reason in my eyes is the Department's future prediction that the children would be at risk if returned to the parent for child neglect—that of not providing consistent medical care. And so, the law has spoken!

I wanted to dedicate this book to the noble foster mother who had enough love to take all three of our babies and nurture them as her own. (That would have given away the ending and so I offer it here). She possesses remarkable and virtuous qualities, she and her husband have opened their hearts to all of us. She consistently keeps us updated with pertinent information as well as pictures and has gotten Sunny and I cleared for visitation! We are now able to see the children on a regular basis and we are considered "family" to her. I spoke with Starre because in some ways it seemed that our visiting with her children was a betrayal. She told me that even if she was cleared, she was not sure she would be able to watch someone else bringing up her children. I think she still needs more time to work through the pain that she had blocked during the reunification process and I do believe when her healing becomes manageable, her unconditional love will shine through for her babies. She gave me her blessing, and I have graciously accepted my grandchildren back into my life! Starre had felt in the end that Jamez did not really want to visit with her anymore anyway as it was confirmed that he became highly emotional to just hearing her name, "Mommy Starre." We will never know whether it was due to emotional pain he associated with his birth mother or his fear of losing the only family he could remember at this point. Helen also let me know that she felt it was important for all of us to be a part of their lives. I know in my heart that Helen has completely devoted her life to giving children the best possible upbringing imaginable. Thank you so very much!

Helen and her devoted husband officially adopted the three children on July 25, 2017.

CHAPTER 24

FINAL RANT

Life has become a burden for me. My "I can do it" mantra has a new focus. That of keeping myself so busy that I have little time to think, to dwell on what could have been.

Days fade into months and years have passed by. The time lost with my children is so precious and so traumatizing to me. While I use to love to see the pictures and videos that Helen sent of my amazing children, I can't help but be so broken-hearted as to all I am missing. I gaze into their tender faces and feel so empty. An emptiness that will always be a part of me. [I can only hope that this vacancy will eventually be filled with God's pure love, while repelling the fear, anger and bitterness that try to seep in.]

My free moments give me time to wonder. This is not a casual wondering, but a woeful and necessary wondering in hopes of freeing and releasing the structure society creates and I follow. [Forgiveness is just a word until you actually have to do it; as that is the only way to let go and move forward in life.]

I grew up respecting nature, my dad passing down his culture as part Blackfoot Indian. As a family, hiking, canoeing, and camping were often partaken. It was our upbringing and heritage. This type of cultivating led me to be spiritually inclined with nature. Along with this heritage, my mother blessed me with the knowledge of angels and other celestial leads.

When my children were taken, I was tried in the harshest way possible. They took my spirituality to court! They took my beliefs LITERALLY! They took my beliefs and compared them to LAW! Lastly, aside from my beliefs, they took my HUMAN NATURE and cut my learning experience—terminating my parental rights forever!

Who's the perpetrator? There has got to be a better way to help individuals to make families foundationally stronger and give people opportunities to make choices that are respected and fulfilling. As a give and take, bargain or compromise, "I do this—you give me that." Yes, instant gratification because that's the way the world currently operates. If I really want my children and you don't like their father because he is not participating in your legal game, it's not ethical to take them from a caring, dedicated mother just because you don't have enough support to foster our relationship intensely.

I was judged by the courts saying my beliefs were whimsical. Okay, why are you *now using "fortune telling" to predict my future? I am not everybody else. I change, I learn, I grow. So sorry, but me being a "nice person" and giving people chances got my children taken away? Just because I allow room for feeling out situations before I cut people off. Just because I don't judge and was still growing in knowing that judging could be ethical for a healthy and balanced life? This kindness and willingness to accept and or help another person got my children taken away? Can you "see" that being in love does not consciously allow the obvious?*

A healthy relationship?!! Look at the United States of America for a role model!! Look at our *relationship—DHHS and myself. They found something as small as letting my child taste a hot chip to say I was improperly feeding him at my fully supervised visit! Talk about making me walk on eggshells; nitpicking my every move!*

Are you kidding me? Do you really think that I would not protect my children when that is what I have done from the very beginning? I was quoted

160

as being "overprotective" at the hospital when Zoe was born! What did you expect? I have more will power and adrenaline strength than a raging dinosaur!! I would die for my children and almost did! The thought of taking my own life was so close to becoming far more than a thought many times during this so called "reunification" process. The idea that I wasn't needed when you took away my motherhood was viciously overwhelming for me. I actually think back and wonder how I did it and how I still do it.

When you have children with someone, does that relationship just fade away? My first child taken after seven months; don't you think that might take a few years before we could fully let go and separate? It didn't help taking away my learning experience!! I would have left the father even sooner if I was to see first-hand his actions as a serious threat to my son. The kick here is that I did see a potential threat, fortunately my son was not hurt but I was in a new relationship that was forming and experiencing the newness of having a child together. At that time, I did indeed believe there was room for chances. We had taken parenting classes that illuminated how important a father's role is in a child's life and based on that psychological factor, I chose to try harder for our child. They never saw it that way...

Nor did they see that each parent is part of their child and therefore should be understood by both parties to best support their children.

Was I judged based on social class as well? Because I did not fit into a category.... I had a prestigious education in graduating from the FIDM, Musicians Institute along with Barbizon of Hollywood. Yet I was living off of assistance and displaced! That probably didn't make much sense. My plan was to be there for my children full time for the major years that shape their foundation—zero to three at least. Along with enriching them with love and education. Okay, a bit of a backroad, but my body was ready to have children and my natural mind was too.

After taking sociology and beginning to study political science, I am wowed by the expectations of society and class and have begun to start to provide for myself; saving up to have a family the right way, some day. I shut off the struggle and found a way to find happiness within it and they shot me down. They took everything from me! My children were my pride and joy and they took them!! My gift, to watch enrich the world with their beauty.